OP
AI!

HELENA AND VIKKI MOURSELLAS

OPA!

RECIPES inspired by
GREEK TAVERNAS

Smith Street Books

Contents

Introduction
6

Our Greek pantry
12

Appetisers
16

From the oven
128

From the sea
62

Vegetables
164

Meat
102

A treat to finish
192

Cheers to us
222

THANK YOU
248

INDEX
250

INTRODUCTION

" 'OPA' is a phrase that captures the warmth of Greek culture"

YASOU, HELENA AND VIKKI HERE. We are back ... and yes, we did say that our last cookbook *Peináo* wasn't 'another Greek taverna cookbook' – well, guess what? This one is. *OPA!* is filled with recipes inspired by our love of traditional Greek tavernas and the food they serve. Firstly, thank you for giving *OPA!* a home in your kitchen – it means the world to us.

'Opa' is a phrase that captures the warmth of Greek culture, and it's an expression that carries many meanings depending on the context it's used in. It can be an expression of joy or excitement in social settings such as weddings or festivals. It could be shouted out to encourage or congratulate someone when they perform a dance move or achieve something of importance as a way to cheer them on. 'Opa' is often yelled when someone starts plate smashing – an ancient tradition that some Greeks (mostly the older generation) see as a stereotype, but still features at celebrations like weddings and christenings – but it could also be said if someone simply drops something accidentally. In an unexpected moment, it can be said to acknowledge someone's surprise like, 'OPA, you didn't marry a Greek man?'

This book is our collection of recipes that reflect the heart of Greek food. It is a book of humble and simple dishes that hold special memories for us, alongside recipes that are inspired by meals we have enjoyed at tavernas across Greece. Naming the book *OPA!* felt fitting because it's a word that captures the joy and celebration that is at the core of Greek food culture. For Greeks, food is about more than just recipes; it's about the memories shared around a table, where meals are eaten slowly, conversations flow freely, and every mouthful is an opportunity to connect. The ambiance, the smell of the dishes wafting through the air, the lively conversations – and let's not forget a shot of ouzo – all create a moment that's deeply ingrained in the Greek way of life. All of this, for us, is captured in the word 'opa'.

For many people around the world, ourselves included, visiting Greece often means falling in love with its food. Whether in bustling cities like Athens or Thessaloniki, or the islands, Greeks embody a deep appreciation for food and the rituals that surround it, and the taverna is often at the heart of this. During our own journeys through Greece over the years, we've had the pleasure of discovering classic recipes and witnessing the traditional taverna experience evolve through modern times.

INTRODUCTION

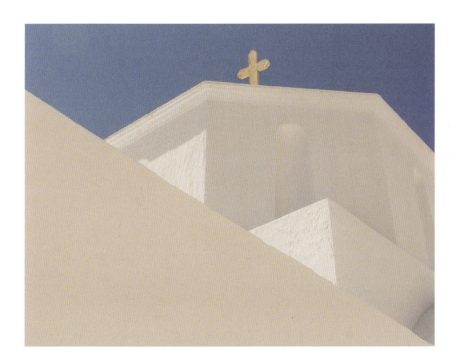

OPA!

INTRODUCTION

> "These evenings were about more than eating; they were the moments where our love for entertaining and connecting with people blossomed"

Our first trip to Greece was in 1994 at the age of six. Mum had not been back since she was 19 years old and was keen to visit her family, so she packed our bags and off we went to Greece for the summer. Her mother, our yiayia Koula, was born in Halkidiki, a region in northern Greece known for its stunning peninsulas and Mediterranean forests. In the 1990s, Mum's first cousin Chris and his wife Eleni owned a taverna right in the heart of their village, which they ran from the front of their house. Eleni, a self-taught cook, did all the cooking herself. Her food was traditional and humble.

We spent evenings at their taverna perched on the bar stools, requesting endless glasses of lemonade and bowls of Eleni's famous fried potatoes with Chicken souvlaki (page 106). By the end of the first night, we were eager to help out. We would clear plates from tables and introduce ourselves to everyone as the 'twins from Australia'. These evenings were about more than eating; they were the moments where our love for entertaining and connecting with people blossomed. Being Sagittarians probably helped – we weren't shy at all, and Mum had to pull us out of there to get us home to sleep. When we arrived back in Australia Dad said to Mum that our routine was out the window. There was no more staying up until midnight, drinking unlimited soda and eating Nutella crepes (oh to be six again!).

While tavernas are often associated with picturesque scenes from the countryside and islands, there are also tavernas in the cities. In Athens and Thessaloniki, tavernas can be found in various neighbourhoods, especially in older parts of the city where there is a strong cultural heritage. Our aunty Christine has lived in Thessaloniki for 30 years and knows where to find all the hidden gems.

Regardless of whether they are in the city, on the islands or in the countryside, tavernas all approach food and cooking with simplicity. Chefs prioritise using locally grown vegetables and fruit, freshly caught seafood, and olive oil and olives sourced from the markets or nearby farms. The recipes most chefs serve are traditional and have been passed down through generations, and the menus can vary depending on the location of the taverna. A coastal taverna in Naxos or Crete might serve freshly caught octopus or fish, while tavernas in mountainous regions are known to cook hearty stews such as Katsikaki tsigariasto (page 162), using local meats and vegetables. Cooking methods are simple – grilling over charcoal, slow braising and baking in clay pots are some common techniques the Greeks have been using for generations, and they play a big part in giving these dishes their classic flavours and textures.

> "Whether you are eating in a taverna or at home, parea (company) is just as important as the food you are eating"

As part of writing this book, Helena journeyed to Greece with our mum, Sophie, in a quest to uncover some of the country's best tavernas and to seek inspiration that would eventually find its way into *OPA!* Along the way, Helena immersed herself in the local culture, built connections with taverna regulars and engaged in heartfelt conversations with the owners. She even received a few cherished recipes from the chefs. Scattered throughout the chapters of this book are profiles of some of these tavernas and their owners. These encounters and culinary stories from tavernas across Greece are lovingly shared, each recipe a tribute to the rich flavours and traditions that define Greek cuisine. Helena's travels not only celebrate the food, but also honour the hospitality and community spirit that thrives within Greece's beloved tavernas.

The chapters in this book reflect the menus of tavernas all over Greece. We start off with appetisers, then seafood, meat dishes, oven-baked classics and vegetables, before moving on to desserts and finishing off – of course – with very delicious drinks. Each recipe in *OPA!* tells a story and offers a taste of Greece that we hope will inspire you to create memorable moments in your own kitchen. From Beef pastitsio with graviera bechamel (page 145) to Sardines with tomato and marjoram (page 71), this book invites you to embrace the joy of cooking and to share meals with the ones you love.

Whether you are eating in a taverna or at home, parea (company) is just as important as the food you are eating, and the Greeks love inviting anyone and everyone to their table to share in their warm hospitality. They welcome guests like family, which is why people keep coming back. The relaxed atmosphere makes you feel at home. We hope *OPA!* can bring that same happiness into your kitchen and that our recipes will come to be loved by you and your favourite people.

Before you get started, remember to enjoy cooking, pour that glass of ouzo, and dance around your kitchen table like no one is watching.

OPA!

Helena and Vikki xx

INTRODUCTION

OUR GREEK PANTRY

A WELL-STOCKED PANTRY MAKES anyone a better cook, and we believe that having basic ingredients stored away for those moments when the fridge or pantry is running low makes life a bit easier. We tend to shop like our grandparents did, buying in bulk and shopping for seasonal produce as much as we can. Their laundry cupboards would always be stocked with tins of tomatoes and beans, packets of pasta, rice and tomato passata (pureed tomatoes) – almost like a mini supermarket! Most Greek recipes use everyday ingredients, so you are more than likely to have all the basics you need to cook from *OPA!* These are our must-have ingredients.

OIL

Life without olive oil sounds a little sad. Let's be honest, we are olive oil snobs; we blame our yiayia for this. She would only cook with Greek olive oil, which she would buy from her local Greek deli. The Greeks consume the most olive oil in the world per capita – which isn't surprising considering Greece produces the purest and most delicious olive oil, as it has for centuries, with the oldest living olive tree being about 3000 years old. We use olive oil that comes from Greece and Australia, as both countries produce beautiful oil. Extra virgin olive oil is the best to use for finishing a dish, like drizzling over lemony mussels or a Dakos salad (page 178). For baking, we like to use a light olive oil, and sometimes extra virgin olive oil, depending on the dish. For shallow-frying, we use a light olive oil or vegetable oil. If you can, try purchasing Greek olive oil; you can really taste the difference.

SALT

We use fine salt for cooking, and good-quality salt flakes for seasoning (with Maldon sea salt flakes being our favourite). Since we all have different tastebuds, it's crucial to taste as you cook to ensure you achieve the perfect balance.

VINEGAR

In our kitchen, we swear by a red wine vinegar made solely from Greek red wine. Its tart and vibrant flavour profile lifts salad dressings and pickles. Greek red wine vinegar is readily available from most European supermarkets.

PITA BREAD

Yes, making your own pita bread is always rewarding (see page 26), but we know how busy life can be. Having a packet of good-quality pita breads stashed in your freezer is truly life-changing when unexpected guests turn up. Throw a pita in a chargrill pan over high heat, combine dried oregano with olive oil and brush it over the pita bread once cooked. Perfect for scooping up Melitzanosalata (page 25).

OUR GREEK PANTRY

LEMONS

Lemons play a significant role in Greek cooking, adding a citrusy flavour and brightness to many dishes. Freshly squeezed lemon juice is a great way to season or marinate meat, fish and vegetables as it adds a tangy flavour that also helps tenderise meats. We grew up with a lemon and a mandarin tree, and picking fresh citrus from them in winter was truly magical, their flavour was unlike any supermarket lemon or mandarin we had ever tasted. Our papou Vasilis was a painter and artist and we would drag his painting ladder to the trees to pick all the fruit.

GREEK OREGANO

The most quintessential herb in Greek cooking is oregano, both dried and fresh. Its robust and distinctive flavour pairs beautifully with dishes like Lamb kleftiko (page 150), moussaka and Beef pastitsio (page 145), as well as vegetables and salad dressings. It has a different flavour from any other oregano grown in Europe. The mountain oregano that has the stems attached is dried naturally and contains important aromatic and nutritional qualities; you can find this type in most European delis. Our yiayia's sister Aleka grows her own oregano in the village, and dries it in the laundry. To dry your own oregano at home, simply tie bunches of fresh oregano with string and hang them upside down in a shady place for 2–3 weeks. When dried, the leaves should be brittle.

HERBS

Greeks love their parsley and dill, which are mostly used fresh. Growing your own herbs can be such a treat, if you have the garden space, although potted herbs like basil are easy to grow on a sunny windowsill. Dill is widely used in Greek cooking, particularly with seafood dishes, dips such as Tzatziki (page 114), and in salads, as its mild, slightly liquorice-like flavour complements fish and vegetables beautifully. Dried mint, parsley, basil, thyme and bay leaves are always great to have in your pantry for when you don't have fresh herbs to use.

HONEY

Known for its intense and complex flavours, Greek honey is considered to be some of the finest in the world, and if you have travelled to Greece you will know that honey holds a special place in Greek culture. The varieties we love to use are thyme honey, pine honey and wildflower honey. The best way to eat honey is poured over thick Greek-style yoghurt – and of course in desserts such as our Loukoumades (page 199).

OLIVES

Different regions produce olives with varying flavour profiles due to the differences in climate, soil and cultivation practices. We never ate olives growing up, as we weren't fans of them – but as adults we cannot live without them. There's always a jar of olives in our fridge, often ones from Thessaloniki, or our yiayia's village of Halkidiki in northern Greece, and it's handy to have a jar of Kalamata olives in the pantry. For a quick mezze, place the olives in a baking dish along with some olive oil, fennel seeds, fresh rosemary sprigs and strips of lemon and orange peel and place into a 200°C (400°F) oven for 20 minutes, or until the olives are warm and fragrant. Serve warm.

LEGUMES

Legumes play a big part in the Greek diet and are considered to be the secret to longevity. Our pantry is always filled with some kind of dried legume. Yiayia would make us our favourite soups, especially during winter, including fakes, a lentil and vegetable soup, and fasolada, a hearty bean soup with white beans, tomatoes and fresh herbs. Our Grilled calamari with fava and pickled onion dish (page 78) is a great way to use yellow split peas.

CHEESE

Greek cheeses can be found in most supermarkets. Among non-Greeks, the most popular is feta – a crumbly and salty cheese made with sheep's milk, and sometimes a blend of sheep's and goat's milk.

Resembling thick yoghurt in texture, galotyri is a soft and creamy curd cheese with a pleasing acidic taste and a delicious milky finish. See page 118 for our Honey chicken wings with galotyri and green pepper herby oil.

Graviera is a semi-hard yellow cheese with a nutty and fruity flavour. It's very popular in Greece where it's used for grating over pasta or in pitas, or as an option for saganaki (pan-fried cheese).

Traditionally made in Cyprus using sheep's and goat's milk, haloumi has a tangy, salty flavour and a texture that could be described as 'squeaky', with a high melting point.

Kasseri is a traditional pale yellow cheese known for its mild taste, made from unpasteurised sheep's milk and occasionally goat's milk. It has a semi-hard to hard consistency, smooth texture and buttery flavour.

Kefalotyri is a hard salty cheese made from sheep's milk. It has a firm, dry texture and strong, tangy flavour. Our papou Vasilis would eat slices of kefalotyri with olives and his dark ale beer, and this cheese reminds us of him.

Manouri is a creamy, semi-soft cheese made from sheep's or goat's milk whey, and is a by-product of feta making. Produced in northern regions of Greece, it's enjoyed as a dessert cheese (served with honey or fruit) and in savoury dishes, such as salads, pies or grilled as part of an appetiser.

Mizithra is made from sheep's or goat's milk whey, it is mild but slightly tangy, similar to Italian ricotta salata. It is perfect for grating or crumbling on top of pasta or salads.

APPETISERS

OPEKTIKA

Ordering appetisers is where the fun begins at every taverna. As soon as the menu appears, everyone eagerly voices their must-have mezze plate. It might be irresistibly crunchy Kolokithakia kai melitzanes tiganites (page 60), fiery Tirokafteri (page 20), or any number of region-specific fritters – on the island of Tinos, the fritters are all about fennel, while on nearby Sifnos, the fritters celebrate the island's famed chickpeas (page 42). Before you know it, an empty table transforms into a vibrant mosaic of plates of all sizes, carafes of house wine, torn bits of fresh bread scattered about, and the occasional rogue fried potato.

Some dishes are seasonal treasures, like the locally caught and pickled octopus at our favourite taverna, Takis, on Fourka Beach in Halkidiki – it's one of the best dishes to eat in the summer. And while you can enjoy a horiatiki (Greek salad) any time of the year, Greek tomatoes reach their sweetest, juiciest peak during summer.

In the sun-drenched summer months, Greeks usually have their main meal of the day around 3 pm. It might seem early at first, but you'll be surprised how quickly you get used to this rhythm, which often includes a cheeky late-afternoon siesta.

APPETISERS

TIROKAFTERI
Spicy cheese dip
20

RYE CONFIT GARLIC TARAMOSALATA
22

MELITZANOSALATA
Eggplant and roasted red peppers
25

PITA BREADS WITH CONFIT
GARLIC OIL
26

TUNA WITH BLOOD ORANGE &
SHALLOT VINAIGRETTE
28

DOLMADES
Lamb-stuffed vine leaves
31

PATATES TIGANITES
Greek fries with goat's feta
and oregano
34

TAVERNA DIARIES:
TAVERNA TOU CHARIS, NAXOS -
PATATES ME AVGA
Potato and eggs with graviera
36

REVITHOKEFTEDES
Chickpea fritters with
minty yoghurt
42

STUFFED FRIED OLIVES
45

FILO-FRIED FETA WITH
HONEY & NUTS
46

BOUYIOURDI
Baked feta with tomato and peppers
48

TAVERNA DIARIES:
STA FYS' AERA, TINOS -
KAGIANAS
Eggs with artichoke and tomato
52

HORIATIKO PSOMI
Black olive village bread
59

KOLOKITHAKIA KAI
MELITZANES TIGANITES
Fennel-seed fried zucchini
and eggplant
60

TIROKAFTERI
Spicy cheese dip

Tirokafteri – literally translating to 'spicy cheese' – is a dip that always finds its way onto our taverna table. Different regions have their own variations, and while most use feta, creamier cheeses such as manouri can also be used. A similar dip, htipiti, is made with feta, roasted red peppers (capsicums) and red chilli, making it a bit spicier (for a milder flavour, simply omit the chilli). Tirokafteri is endlessly versatile and makes a perfect pasta sauce when stirred through some pasta, such as makaronia. Try this and thank us later.

It's no secret that in Greece, you'll find incredibly creamy Greek yoghurt. To achieve this at home for your dips, strain 500 g (2 cups) of yoghurt overnight. Simply place it in a cheesecloth-lined strainer over a bowl, cover with a tea towel, and leave in the fridge overnight. The next morning, discard the whey at the bottom of the bowl and store the thickened yoghurt in an airtight container. It's ready to use!

Crumble the feta into a food processor. Add the olive oil, lemon juice, yoghurt and chilli. Blitz for a few seconds until combined; you want the mixture slightly chunky, but smooth.

Spread onto a serving plate and top with a black olive and a drizzle of olive oil.

Makes 410 g (1½ cups)

- 250 g (9 oz) Greek feta
- 60 ml (¼ cup) extra virgin olive oil, plus extra to serve
- 1 tablespoon lemon juice
- 80 g (2¾ oz) thick Greek-style yoghurt
- 1 long red chilli, chopped
- 1 black olive

A NOTE ON PREP
This dip can be made the day before and stored in an airtight container in the fridge for up to 1 week. Tirokafteri will harden when refrigerated, so remove it from the fridge before serving and give it a good stir so it's creamy.

SERVE ME WITH
Slices of fresh bread, olives, brined caper leaves and sardines - and wash it all down with a glass of ouzo over ice.

APPETISERS

RYE CONFIT GARLIC TARAMOSALATA

We haven't always been obsessed with tarama. Only in our adult years have we really appreciated its flavour. If you don't like fishy flavours, this dip is not for you. You will find tarama caviar at fishmongers and specialty stores; it's usually made with mullet roe that has been blended into a paste.

There are two types of ready-made tarama spreads on the market: the pink version that's sold at supermarkets, which has a subtle fish flavour and uses potato; and white tarama, which has a stronger flavour and is made using soaked stale bread.

We have used rye bread here because we find the malt flavour complements the tarama. Different toppings are always nice, we like to add salmon caviar with a drizzle of olive oil, a black olive or a sprinkle of paprika. If you are short on time, skip the confit garlic and simply drizzle with a flavoured olive oil.

In case you're wondering what the ice cubes do, they help give the tarama a light and fluffy texture.

Makes 500 g (1 lb 2 oz)

100 g (3½ oz) tarama caviar
2 Confit garlic cloves (page 26), plus a couple to serve; alternatively, use 1 crushed garlic clove
70 g (2½ oz) stale rye bread, crusts removed, torn into small chunks
250 ml (1 cup) light olive oil, plus an extra 2 tablespoons if using confit garlic
6 small ice cubes
2 tablespoons lemon juice
salt flakes

Place the caviar and confit garlic (or crushed garlic) in a food processor and blend until smooth.

Place the bread in a small bowl and cover with water, then drain and squeeze out the excess water.

Add the bread to the food processor and continue blending until smooth. With the motor running, gradually add the olive oil in a slow, steady stream until the mixture emulsifies. Add the ice cubes, one by one, and process until completely blended and silky smooth.

Add the lemon juice, season with salt flakes and mix to combine.

In a bowl, mash the extra confit garlic cloves with an extra 2 tablespoons of olive oil.

Spoon the tamara onto a serving plate and top with the confit garlic oil mixture.

A NOTE ON PREP
The taramosalata can be made the day before and stored in an airtight container in the fridge for up to 1 week. The flavour will continue to develop with time.

SERVE ME WITH
Scoop up the taramosalata with some warm pita bread (page 26) and enjoy with a glass of retsina or dry white wine.

APPETISERS

APPETISERS

MELITZANOSALATA
Eggplant and roasted red peppers

Spiked with garlic, fresh parsley, lemon juice and extra virgin olive oil, melitzanosalata is a lovely mezze to serve with warm pita bread (page 26). Cooking eggplant over an open flame will give your melitzanosalata a smoky flavour and creamy interior.

If cooking on an open flame isn't an option, you can achieve a similar flavour by baking the eggplants in a 200°C (400°F) oven. Coat in some olive oil, sprinkle with salt and roast for 1 hour, or until the skin is slightly darkened.

Makes 600 g (2½ cups)

- 2 large eggplants (aubergines), about 850 g (1 lb 14 oz) in total
- 1 red pepper (capsicum)
- vegetable oil, for shallow-frying
- 2 pita breads, cut into large wedges
- 1 small red onion, finely chopped
- 1 garlic clove, crushed
- ¼ bunch of parsley, finely chopped
- zest of 1 lemon, plus 2 tablespoons lemon juice
- 125 ml (½ cup) extra virgin olive oil, plus extra for drizzling
- 1 teaspoon salt flakes
- freshly cracked black pepper

Carefully place a small flame-resistant rack over an open flame set to medium heat. Place the whole eggplants on the rack and cook for 15–20 minutes, rotating the eggplants occasionally, until dry and blackened on the outside, and soft in the middle. Set aside until cool enough to handle, then slice the eggplants in half and place them in a sieve over a bowl to allow any excess liquid to drain out.

Pierce the red pepper with a skewer and place over the open flame for 15 minutes, turning occasionally, until softened and charred. Place in a bowl, cover with plastic wrap and leave to sweat for 20 minutes. The charred skin should now pull away from the flesh easily.

Heat 1 cm (½ in) vegetable oil in a large saucepan until the oil reaches 180°C (350°F) on a kitchen thermometer. Fry the pita bread wedges in batches for 2 minutes on each side, until golden brown and crispy. Drain on paper towel.

Using a large spoon, scoop out the flesh from the eggplant into a bowl, then mash with a fork. Chop the red pepper and add to the bowl. Stir in the remaining ingredients, season and drizzle with a little extra olive oil to serve.

A NOTE ON PREP
To enhance the smoky flavour, make the melitzanosalata the day before; it will keep covered in the fridge for up to 1 week.

Any leftovers are best served on top of a slice of our Horiatiko psomi on page 59 as an easy appetiser or lunch for one.

SERVE ME WITH
Chicken souvlaki with Greek fries (page 106).

PITA BREADS WITH CONFIT GARLIC OIL

Makes 8

2 teaspoons active dried yeast
1 teaspoon caster (superfine) sugar
250 ml (1 cup) lukewarm water
450 g (3 cups) plain (all-purpose) flour, sifted
2 teaspoons salt flakes
2 tablespoons extra virgin olive oil
olive oil spray

CONFIT GARLIC OIL
250 g (9 oz) peeled garlic cloves, or 3 whole garlic bulbs, peeled
375 ml (1½ cups) extra virgin olive oil
3 lemon thyme sprigs

As much as we love to buy pita bread, it really is so nice to make your own, especially when the smell of freshly fried pita wafts through the house. This recipe is also vegan and perfect for Lent.

To make the confit garlic oil, place the garlic cloves in a saucepan with the olive oil. Place over high heat until the oil reaches 60°C (140°F) on a kitchen thermometer, then reduce the heat to low and cook gently for 30 minutes, or until the garlic is soft and lightly coloured. Remove from the heat.

Allow the garlic oil to completely cool in the pan, then stir the lemon thyme through. Gently pour into a 600 ml (20½ fl oz) sterilised jar and seal with a lid.

To make the pita breads, place the yeast, sugar and lukewarm water in a bowl and set aside for 5 minutes, or until frothy.

Place the flour and salt flakes in the bowl of a stand mixer with the dough hook attached. Pour in the yeast mixture and the olive oil and knead on low speed for 10 minutes, or until a smooth and soft dough forms.

Transfer the dough to a lightly greased bowl and cover with a clean tea towel. Set aside at room temperature for 1 hour, or until the dough has doubled in size.

Knock back the dough, then divide it into 8 pieces. Form into 15 cm (6 in) circles using a floured rolling pin. Keep the rolled dough covered with a tea towel while you fry the pita.

Place a frying pan over high heat and spray with olive oil. Working in batches, fry the pita breads for 2–3 minutes, until they are lightly charred and bubbles start to form. Flip and cook for another 2–3 minutes. Remove from the pan and serve warm with the confit garlic and garlic oil.

A NOTE ON PREP
The dough can be made the day before and stored in the fridge, wrapped in plastic wrap. Remove from the fridge 30 minutes before frying as directed above. The confit oil will keep in a sealed jar in the fridge for up to 2 weeks, just make sure that the garlic cloves are completely submerged in the oil. The oil might harden when refrigerated, so take it out a few hours before you serve it.

SERVE ME WITH
The pitas are perfect to use for a gyros, or slice into pieces and serve with any of the dips from pages 20–25.

APPETISERS

TUNA WITH BLOOD ORANGE & SHALLOT VINAIGRETTE

In Greek coastal areas, particularly on islands such as Crete, Santorini and Mykonos, raw tuna is appreciated for its freshness and simplicity – perfect for enjoying during warm weather with a glass of chilled local wine or ouzo.

Here, the fresh blood orange and the acidity from the vinaigrette works perfectly with the tuna, but if blood oranges are out of season you can use oranges instead.

Combine all the vinaigrette ingredients in a non-metallic bowl and season with salt flakes and cracked pepper.

Add the tuna pieces and toss to coat them in the dressing.

Lay the blood orange slices on a serving platter, top with the tuna mixture, season with salt flakes and scatter with a few extra oregano leaves.

Feeds 4

salt flakes and freshly cracked black pepper
1 × 300 g (10½ oz) sashimi-grade tuna fillet, diced
2 small blood oranges, peeled and finely sliced

BLOOD ORANGE & SHALLOT VINAIGRETTE
2 shallots, finely diced
2 teaspoons white wine vinegar
2 tablespoons extra virgin olive oil
1 tablespoon fresh oregano leaves, plus extra to serve
1 tablespoon blood orange juice

A NOTE ON PREP
The tuna is best served on the day of purchase. You can prepare the vinaigrette the day before and place it in a jar in the fridge.

SERVE ME WITH
For a summer feast, serve the tuna alongside Octopus with caperberries and lemon (page 68) and a Maroulosalata (page 171).

APPETISERS

DOLMADES
Lamb-stuffed vine leaves

You'll find many variations of stuffed vine leaves across Greece, Egypt, Turkey and Lebanon. Some are cooked on the stovetop, others in the oven, and they're typically stuffed with rice, fresh herbs, warm spices, and sometimes minced (ground) lamb or beef, all simmered in a lemony broth. Our version is inspired by the flavours we've enjoyed in Greece.

You can use fresh vine leaves, foraged from your garden or sourced from Greek neighbours, or vacuum-sealed ones from a European deli. Fresh leaves are best picked in late spring to early summer, while they're still tender. Blanch fresh leaves in boiling water for 1 minute, then cool and drain them in a colander. Shop-bought leaves should be soaked in cold water for 30 minutes to remove the excess salt, then patted dry. Damaged leaves can be used to line the bottom of the saucepan.

Makes 38-40

- 80 ml (⅓ cup) extra virgin olive oil
- 1 white onion, finely chopped
- 3 garlic cloves, finely chopped
- 250 g (9 oz) minced (ground) lamb
- 1 teaspoon dried mint
- salt flakes
- 200 g (1 cup) medium-grain white rice, washed well
- 2 tomatoes, about 200 g (7 oz) in total, grated
- ¼ bunch of dill, finely chopped
- ¼ bunch of parsley, finely chopped
- 1 × 500 g (1 lb 2 oz) packet vine leaves, washed and dried well
- 2 tablespoons lemon juice

Place a frying pan over medium heat, add 60 ml (¼ cup) of the olive oil and saute the onion and garlic for about 5 minutes, until softened. Add the lamb and dried mint, season with salt flakes and cook for a further 5 minutes. Add the rice, tomatoes, dill and parsley and saute for a further 5 minutes.

Pour 375 ml (1½ cups) boiling water into the rice mixture, reduce the heat and place a lid on top. Simmer for 8-10 minutes, until the water has been absorbed and the rice is half cooked. Set aside to cool completely.

Prepare your vine leaves following the instructions in the introduction, reserving any broken vine leaves for lining the base of your saucepan. To roll the dolmades, spread the vine leaves, smooth side down, on a work surface. Place 1 tablespoon of the rice mixture at the stem end of each leaf. Fold the edge of the leaf closest to you over the filling and then fold the two side edges inwards, encasing the filling. Tightly roll the vine leaf away from you to form a tight parcel. Repeat with the remaining vine leaves and rice mixture.

Line a 22 cm (8¾ in) cast-iron saucepan with the reserved vine leaves. Place the dolmades snugly in the pan, making two layers.

Make a stock by combining the lemon juice with the remaining olive oil and 250 ml (1 cup) boiling water. Pour over the dolmades.

Place a small heatproof plate on top of the stuffed vine leaves, then place the lid on the pan. Simmer over low heat for 40-45 minutes, until the dolmades are tender.

Allow to cool for 30 minutes in the pan before serving.

A NOTE ON PREP
This is a great mezze to have in the fridge for when unexpected guests arrive, or you can prepare the dolmades a couple of days before a dinner party. They will keep in an airtight container in the fridge for up to 1 week; the flavour will develop over time.

SERVE ME WITH
The dolmades can be served warm or cold with Tzatziki (page 114) and lemon wedges, or with our Rye confit garlic taramosalata (page 22).

PATATES TIGANITES
Greek fries with goat's feta and oregano

On most taverna menus, patates will be the first dish to order – and more often than not, a second (and sometimes third) helping will be ordered.

Every time we smell fried potatoes, it takes us right back to our yiayia Koula's kitchen. It's a truly magical aroma. She always used the best extra virgin olive oil for frying, and would stand by the stove carefully placing piles of sliced potatoes into the hot oil, before placing the freshly fried patates on the table, along with lamb or pork keftedes and a big bowl of garlicky Tzatziki (page 114). Eager to tend to us, she would often serve us watermelon and cantaloupe (rockmelon) while we were still eating.

The best potatoes for these fries are floury ones, such as sebago or russet. We have paired them with goat's feta, as it's one we really enjoy eating, but cow's milk feta is also lovely.

Peel the potatoes and cut into chips about 1 cm (½ in thick). Place in a large bowl, cover with cold water and leave to soak for 30 minutes. (Soaking your potatoes draws out the starch and helps achieve crispier chips during frying.) Drain the potatoes well, thoroughly pat dry with paper towel or a clean tea towel and set aside.

Half-fill a saucepan with olive oil and heat to 180°C (350°F) on a kitchen thermometer. Deep-fry the potatoes in batches for 3–4 minutes, until golden and crispy. Drain on paper towel to remove any excess oil.

Season the potatoes with the oregano and salt flakes and crumble the feta over.

Feeds 4

1 kg (2 lb 3 oz) roasting potatoes, such as russet or sebago
olive oil, for deep-frying
1 teaspoon dried Greek oregano
salt flakes
60 g (2 oz) goat's feta

A NOTE ON PREP
Patates tiganites are best fried to order.

SERVE ME WITH
A feast with our Pork chops with roasted pepper butter (page 108) and a Horiatiki salata (page 168).

APPETISERS

In a serene village called
Eggares, on the island of
Naxos, lies this charming
family-run taverna. Located at
the entrance of the village,
TAVERNA TOU CHARIS is very
well known for its warm
hospitality and signature
dish: a 15-egg omelette with
potatoes and graviera cheese.
Many locals and tourists claim
the taverna serves the best
home-cooked meals on Naxos.

When we arrived and ordered the omelette, we were told it was big enough to feed up to six people. Its height and fluffiness was something we had never encountered before. You can tell the eggs are local, the colour of the yolks a vibrant yellow. We were also told we couldn't leave without trying the rabbit slow-cooked in lemon and olive oil. It turned out to be the most delicate, delicious rabbit we have ever eaten! The rabbit was falling off the bone and covered in a sour lemon sauce, coating the accompanying potatoes with all the juices. It was one of those dishes you dream of. Their lamb fricassee is similarly adored.

The taverna came to life in 1977, but its story really dates back to 1969, when its owner, Evgenia Arseni, began working after school at a traditional butcher-style taverna. She was very young at the time, but eager to learn - carefully observing the cook, taking in as much information as she could and collecting some of their recipes in secret. A few years later, Evgenia and her husband, Charis, became the new owners of that taverna, because the original owners had to relocate to Athens. However, in 1977 they decided to build their own taverna and bought this beautiful piece of land in Eggares - a serene village described by the famous Greek writer Nikos Kazantzakis as 'paradise on earth'.

All the dishes that are cooked in the taverna are from their own home-grown or locally sourced ingredients - their rabbits, roosters and hens are served alongside their freshly harvested vegetables. Evgenia and Charis' dedication to quality and their personal touch helped them establish a name for themselves pretty quickly, their taverna quickly became a beloved spot for locals and tourists. Today people travel from all over the world to sample the taverna's delicious meals.

TAVERNA TOU CHARIS

> "The chemistry of the whole family, in combination with the exceptional food, makes you feel at home as soon as you step into the taverna"

Even though the taverna takes her husband's name, 'Charis', Evgenia is its backbone. Evgenia is one of the main cooks there, and her recipes are relished by many. When we arrived at the taverna she was serving and waiting tables, explaining the menu to guests with passion and excitement; it was such a beautiful sight. When I asked if I could take her photo she was more than happy to stand by the door, smiling proudly, and she joined us later in the night to sit with us and share her story. Moments like these make us feel grateful to have found Evgenia and her family - they were so welcoming and made us feel like we were in their home.

Everything is cooked to perfection, with Evgenia in the kitchen, and Charis being master of the rotisserie, grilling ribs, burgers and sausages from three different meats - goat, beef and pork - all grown on their farm. The chemistry of the whole family, in combination with the exceptional food, makes you feel at home as soon as you step into the taverna.

Evgenia's son Spyros has a natural talent for cooking both his own recipes and his mother's traditional dishes. It seems he's well on his way to becoming the next generation to run the family taverna.

The taverna kindly shared with us their popular potato omelette recipe. They actually use 15 eggs in theirs, but have given us a version using 10 eggs, to make it more practical for a home kitchen.

PATATES ME AVGA
Potato and eggs with graviera

Feeds 4-6

800 g (1 lb 12 oz) potatoes
250 ml (1 cup) olive oil
200 g (7 oz) graviera cheese, cut into 2 cm (¾ in) chunks
10 eggs, lightly beaten

Peel the potatoes and cut into chips about 1 cm (½ in) thick and 8 cm (3¼ in) long. Place in a large bowl, cover with cold water and leave to soak for 30 minutes. (Soaking your potatoes draws out the starch and helps achieve crispier chips during frying.) Drain well, thoroughly pat dry with paper towel or a clean tea towel and set aside.

Pour the olive oil into a deep-sided 22 cm (8¾ in) non-stick frying pan and heat to 180°C (350°F) on a kitchen thermometer. Working in two batches, fry the potatoes for 5–6 minutes, until golden and crispy, and set aside on a plate lined with paper towel to drain.

Remove half the oil from the pan and set aside for another cooking use. Place all the potatoes back in the frying pan and reduce the heat to medium–low.

Scatter the graviera over the potatoes, then cover and allow the cheese to melt for 4–5 minutes. Evenly pour the beaten egg over, put the lid on and cook over low heat for 18–20 minutes, until the edges of the omelette start to brown and the egg is cooked.

Place a plate on top of the omelette and carefully flip it over onto a large serving dish. Slice and serve hot.

A NOTE ON PREP
The potatoes can be cooked a few hours ahead; just make sure you reserve half the olive oil to finish cooking the frittata.

SERVE ME WITH
Any of our meat dishes.

REVITHOKEFTEDES
Chickpea fritters with minty yoghurt

These fritters are one of the most popular mezze on the island of Sifnos. 'Revithi' means 'chickpea' and 'keftedes' is plural for 'keftes', or 'fried ball' – anything fried in olive oil that can be dipped into something creamy is always a favourite!

This recipe uses tinned chickpeas to make it quicker to get these fritters on the table, but feel free to use freshly cooked dried chickpeas. These revithokeftedes can be turned into larger fritters, or could be used as a burger patty. Serve in a soft milk bun with a few slices of ripe tomato, sliced red onion, lettuce leaves and some Tzatziki (page 114), and you have yourself a chickpea burger.

Makes 12

- 400 g (14 oz) tinned chickpeas (garbanzo beans), drained and rinsed
- 1 red onion, roughly chopped
- small handful of roughly chopped parsley
- ¼ teaspoon sweet paprika
- ¼ teaspoon ground cinnamon
- salt flakes and freshly cracked black pepper
- 1 egg, lightly beaten
- 2 tablespoons plain (all-purpose) flour, plus an extra 35 g (¼ cup) for dusting
- 80 ml (⅓ cup) light olive oil

MINTY YOGHURT
- 125 g (½ cup) Greek-style yoghurt
- small handful of chopped mint
- salt flakes

Place half the chickpeas in a food processor with the onion, parsley and spices. Process until roughly chopped. Place the mixture in a bowl with the remaining chickpeas and season to taste with salt flakes and cracked pepper. Stir the egg and 2 tablespoons of flour through until well combined.

Place the extra flour on a plate and line a tray with baking paper. Working with 1 tablespoon of the mixture at a time, shape into balls, then dust in the flour, shaking off any excess flour and placing them on the lined tray.

In a small bowl, combine the yoghurt and mint. Season with salt flakes and set aside for serving.

Heat the olive oil in a large frying pan over medium heat. In batches, cook the fritters for about 5 minutes on each side, until golden and crisp, gently pressing them flat and turning them occasionally. Drain on paper towel and season to taste.

Arrange on a large platter and serve warm, with the minty yoghurt.

A NOTE ON PREP
The fritters are perfectly fine to eat at room temperature. If making them the night before, let them cool completely before storing in a container in the fridge. Reheat in a frying pan over low heat when ready to serve.

SERVE ME WITH
For an afternoon mezze in the sunshine, pair with a glass of cold Greek beer and Fried whitebait with ouzo mayonnaise (page 66).

APPETISERS

43

APPETISERS

STUFFED FRIED OLIVES

It might sound like a lot of work to stuff an olive, but it is so worth it. Appearing on nearly every Greek table, kasseri is a smooth, chewy cheese with a hard rind and a semi-hard to hard consistency. It works so well with the saltiness of the olives – and once coated in a crumb and deep fried, they are so moreish.

Feeds 4-6

180 g (6½ oz) kasseri cheese
36 large green olives, about 180 g (6½ oz), pitted
35 g (¼ cup) plain (all-purpose) flour
salt flakes
2 eggs
75 g (1¼ cups) panko breadcrumbs
vegetable oil, for deep-frying

Slice the kasseri into tiny batons to fit into the slits in the olives, then carefully stuff the olives with the cheese pieces.

Place the flour in a bowl and season with salt flakes. Lightly beat the eggs in another bowl, and place the panko breadcrumbs in a third bowl.

Coat an olive in the flour, followed by the egg, and finally the breadcrumbs. Place on a tray and repeat with the remaining olives.

Half-fill a saucepan with vegetable oil and heat to 180°C (350°F) on a kitchen thermometer. Working in batches, add the olives to the oil and fry for 4–6 minutes, until crispy and golden brown. Remove using a slotted spoon and drain on paper towel to remove any excess oil. Serve hot.

A NOTE ON PREP
The olives can be coated in the crumb mixture the night before and stored in an airtight container in the fridge. The following day, fry the olives using the method above.

SERVE ME WITH
A glass of rose, and a bowl of the Tirokafteri on page 20 to dip the olives into.

FILO-FRIED FETA WITH HONEY & NUTS

Some might say eating a whole block of feta is 'too much cheese for one person'. We totally disagree. Our two great loves are cheese and honey – and here the crispy bits of fried filo pastry pair perfectly with the sweetness of the honey. Traditionally, the Greeks also make a tiropita (cheese pie) which has a cheese and egg filling. Trust us, this simple dish is an absolute treat.

Feeds 2-4

- 200 g (7 oz) block of Greek feta
- 3 sheets filo pastry
- 60 g (2 oz) unsalted butter, melted
- 2 lemon thyme sprigs, leaves picked, plus extra to serve
- 60 ml (¼ cup) olive oil
- 2 tablespoons honey
- 2 tablespoons roasted mixed nuts, roughly chopped
- ½ teaspoon black sesame seeds

Remove the moisture from the feta using paper towel.

Lay a sheet of filo pastry vertically on your kitchen work surface, then brush the entire sheet with melted butter. Stack the remaining two filo pastry sheets, brushing each sheet with butter in between.

Place the block of feta in the centre of the pastry and scatter with the thyme leaves. Fold the pastry over to cover the cheese and brush with more melted butter. Fold the pastry over one last time to enclose. Brush both ends with more melted butter, then fold them over to enclose.

Heat the olive oil in a frying pan over medium heat and fry the pastry parcel for about 3 minutes on each side and on all edges, until crispy and lightly golden on all sides. Remove from the pan and drain on paper towel.

Drizzle the fried feta parcel with the honey, scatter with the nuts, sesame seeds and extra thyme leaves and serve.

A NOTE ON PREP
The filo-fried feta needs to be served straight away, hot from the pan.

SERVE ME WITH
Chop the fried feta into pieces and toss through our Horiatiki salata on page 168 instead of the regular feta.

BOUYIOURDI
Baked feta with tomato and peppers

There are a couple of reasons why we love this dish, one being that it originated in Thessaloniki and the other being that we love a sweet, ripe, summer tomato. Try your best to get your hands on some in-season tomatoes, and if bullhorn peppers aren't available, use a green pepper (capsicum) instead. You can also substitute the kefalotyri cheese with parmesan.

Feeds 4-6

- 450 g (1 lb) cherry tomatoes, chopped
- 2 bullhorn (banana) peppers, finely sliced
- 300 g (10½ oz) Greek feta, crumbled
- 100 g (3½ oz) kefalotyri, grated
- 2 teaspoons dried Greek oregano
- 60 ml (¼ cup) extra virgin olive oil

Preheat the oven to 200°C (400°F).

Scatter the chopped tomatoes in a large baking dish. Top with the bullhorn pepper slices, feta and kefalotyri, sprinkle with the oregano and drizzle with the olive oil. Cover tightly with foil and bake for 30 minutes.

Remove the foil and cook uncovered for a further 15 minutes, or until the cheese is golden brown and gooey. Serve immediately.

A NOTE ON PREP
This dish is best eaten fresh out of the oven. It can be assembled in the baking dish a day ahead and kept in the fridge, ready to cook the following day.

SERVE ME WITH
Spoon onto some fried pita bread (page 26) or toss through freshly cooked buttery makaronia pasta (*sooo* delicious)!

APPETISERS 49

TAVERNA DIARIES

STA FYS' AERA

TINOS

- LOCATION -
Tinos

- ADDRESS -
Aetofolia 842 00, Greece

- PHONE -
+30 2283 051718

- RECIPE -
Kagianas (Eggs with artichoke and tomato)

On the island of Tinos, in the very
small village of Aetofolia, with
a population of only 20 people,
is a charming taverna called
STA FYS' AERA. The village owes
its name to the persistent winds
that sweep through this area. The
taverna has been there since 1938,
but was originally a bakalotaverna,
a cafe and dining space where
locals would drink, shop and eat.
Sadly, the taverna closed in the
1980s - until, in 2012, Nikos
Sklavos, who remembered the taverna
fondly as a kid, decided to bring
it back to life.

Although he has inherited the space, the style, the jukebox, the produce and the spirit and passion with which he manages this taverna is completely his own.

Sta Fys' Aera is well known for its use of fresh vegetables and their amazing meat, primarily sourced from Nikos' farm, but also from friends and other locals on the island. The recipes are truly traditional to the island of Tinos, dating back to the medieval ages, meticulously researched and crafted by Nikos, who has travelled extensively to places such as Athens, Venetia and Geneva and visited their libraries in his quest to understand how the products that were raised on the island were used in its local dishes. After translating ancient texts and reading widely, he created a menu for his taverna that is deeply historical and refreshingly unique.

The taverna works with the same menu all year round. However, the ingredients used for each recipe vary with the seasons. If you visit around Easter, you may enjoy an omelette with garmpia, a wildflower that comes from a special type of cabbage that only flowers at that time of year. If you were to visit in September, however, Nikos would recreate the dish using a white eggplant (aubergine) of Tinos that is a trademark of the island and is only grown there, and the gastronomical experience would of course be very different.

When we visited, Nikos had four different kagianas (scrambled egg) offerings on the menu. Kagianas is a popular dish around the Greek islands, and is often served for lunch or a light snack. The kagianas recipe he kindly shared with us features artichokes, for which the island of Tinos is renowned.

"People come here to drink and discuss, and sometimes they come for a glendi - a Greek party"

More than just a taverna, Sta Fys' Aera is not only about food. People come here to drink and discuss, and sometimes they come for a glendi - a Greek party. Music also plays a big role here. During winter, a bunch of musicians from the island gather to sing together next to the fireplace. Another thing that doesn't go unnoticed is the gorgeous vintage jukebox in the corner. Nikos explains he had always wanted a jukebox ever since he worked abroad, so he could listen to his favourite singers back then: Stavros Xarhakos, Manolis Angelopoulos, Apostolos Kaldaras. One thing is for sure: the taverna and its people know how to have a good time.

For Nikos, the taverna life is about connecting with people, the joy of the community. As he says, he is a captain of a ship, not the boss of people, and he cannot travel on his own. While Nikos works mostly in the kitchen, all the people who work there are part of a team, and that is why it feels like a family - they are all on this journey together.

KAGIANAS
Eggs with artichoke and tomato

Feeds 2

2 tablespoons olive oil
½ red onion, finely chopped
¼ teaspoon sweet paprika, plus extra to serve
salt flakes
1 tomato, roughly chopped
200 g (7 oz) artichoke hearts in oil, drained, halved
¼ cup finely chopped parsley leaves
¼ cup finely chopped dill leaves
2 eggs, lightly beaten
40 g (1½ oz) kefalotyri cheese, grated

Heat the olive oil in a frying pan over medium heat. Add the onion and paprika, season with salt flakes and cook, stirring now and then, for 6 minutes, or until softened and caramelised. Stir in the tomato and artichoke and cook for a further 5 minutes, or until the vegetables have softened slightly. Add the herbs and cook for a further minute.

Add the egg and stir with a spatula for a minute or two, until the egg starts to cook. Top with the grated kefalotyri, sprinkle with extra paprika and serve hot.

A NOTE ON PREP
This is the type of recipe that needs to be cooked just before serving – but feel free to fry the vegetables in advance, then simply finish the dish when you're ready to eat.

SERVE ME WITH
A carb to soak up all those beautiful oily juices. This dish works a treat with our Pita breads with confit garlic oil (page 26) and our Patates tiganites (page 34).

HORIATIKO PSOMI
Black olive village bread

Bread is an essential part of Greek cuisine and a staple on every Greek table. At a taverna, it is usually served as soon as you sit down, sometimes sliced or given as a whole loaf. If you're anything like us, the bread often vanishes before the first small plate even arrives!

Horiatiko psomi, meaning 'village bread', is typically baked in a wood-fired oven, giving it a unique flavour and texture, but we've adapted this recipe for a conventional oven. The bread's crunchy crust and fluffy interior are perfect for soaking up all the zoumi (pan juices) from the recipes in this book.

Makes 1 loaf, enough to feed 6–8

- 450 ml (15 fl oz) lukewarm water
- 7 g sachet (2¼ teaspoons) active dried yeast
- 70 g (½ cup) pitted black olives, chopped
- 650 g (1 lb 7 oz) bread flour, sifted
- 1 tablespoon salt flakes
- 1 tablespoon extra virgin olive oil

In a large jug, combine the lukewarm water and yeast. Set aside for 10 minutes.

Meanwhile, thoroughly dry the olives by placing them on paper towel and pressing down to remove any liquid.

Combine the flour and salt in the bowl of a stand mixer. Add the yeast mixture and olive oil, then knead on low speed for about 10 minutes, until you have a smooth dough. Knead in the olives. Cover with a clean tea towel and leave to prove in a warm spot for 1 hour, or until doubled in size.

Preheat the oven to 230°C (445°F). Place a 22 cm (8¾ in) cast-iron pot in the oven to preheat.

Lift the dough onto a large piece of baking paper and carefully place into the hot cast-iron pot.

Bake for 40–45 minutes, until the loaf is golden and sounds hollow when tapped. Allow to cool slightly before serving.

A NOTE ON PREP
Freshly baked bread is always best enjoyed on the day of baking. If you're short on time, the bread can be baked the night before and left at room temperature, covered with a clean tea towel - or you could bake it in the morning and leave it at room temperature until it's time to serve. Any leftover bread can be sliced and placed in the freezer to enjoy as toast with some Tirokafteri (page 20).

SERVE ME WITH
Absolutely everything!

KOLOKITHAKIA KAI MELITZANES TIGANITES
Fennel-seed fried zucchini and eggplant

This is our post-swim mezze of choice, usually devoured after a power walk from the beach to the taverna, beach towel wrapped around our waists and wet salty hair. Golden, crisp pieces of eggplant and zucchini are a beautiful thing – especially when they've been fried in olive oil. We love the pop of fennel seeds in the batter, but you can omit them if you prefer a plain batter.

Frying the vegetables in a single layer will give you that crisp exterior and a tender, silky and light interior.

Feeds 4-6

- 3 small grey zucchini (courgettes), about 350 g (12½ oz) in total
- 1 eggplant (aubergine), about 500 g (1 lb 2 oz), cut down the middle
- 150 g (1 cup) plain (all-purpose) flour, sifted
- 150 g (5½ oz) cornflour (corn starch), sifted
- 1 tablespoon fennel seeds
- salt flakes and freshly cracked black pepper
- 250 ml (1 cup) cold Greek beer, or any other beer
- 125 ml (½ cup) cold sparkling water
- vegetable oil, for deep-frying

Cut the zucchini and eggplant into slices about 5 mm (¼ in) thick.

In a bowl, combine the flour, cornflour and fennel seeds and season with salt flakes and cracked pepper. Make a well in the centre, then pour in the beer and sparkling water. Whisk until a smooth batter forms.

Heat about 10 cm (4 in) of vegetable oil in a deep-fryer or medium-sized frying pan until the temperature comes to 180°C (350°F) on a kitchen thermometer.

Place the zucchini and eggplant slices into the batter and mix to coat (if the batter is a little runny, add a few sprinkles of flour; but you don't want a thick batter).

Using tongs, and working in batches, pull the vegetables out of the batter and carefully drop them into the hot oil. Cook for 3–4 minutes, until crispy and golden brown. Drain on paper towel, season with salt flakes and serve immediately.

A NOTE ON PREP
These are best served freshly fried. The vegetables can be prepared a couple of hours before and left to sit at room temperature until just before frying.

SERVE ME WITH
Endless dipping options! We love dipping the vegetables into some Greek-style yoghurt with fresh finely chopped garlic and finely chopped parsley stirred through. They're also perfect dipped into Tirokafteri (page 20).

APPETISERS

THE SEA

ΘΑΛΑΣΣΙΝΑ

One of the best things about Greek summers is enjoying a long lunch at a seaside psarotaverna, a fish taverna, especially after a day of soaking up the sun and swimming in the clear blue waters. Every Greek island and coastal town that hugs the Aegean has its fair share of these charming spots, often with octopus tentacles hanging out to dry or a small fishing boat bobbing in the nearby water – a good sign of the morning's fresh catch.

There's an extra advantage to dining during the new or full moon, as these times are said to bring in the best fishing, meaning a wider selection of fish – especially on the smaller islands where the daily catch sets the menu. For a more authentic experience, we like to find the tavernas with a simple menu focused on the day's haul, steering clear of those with lots of options that often include frozen seafood (which will usually be marked with an asterisk on the menu).

In Greece, smaller fish such as barbounia (red mullet, see page 76), sardines and maridaki (whitebait, see page 66) are popular and easy to find. When it comes to seafood, it's hard to beat the taste of freshly fried calamari, prawn (shrimp) saganaki bubbling in a rich tomato sauce, or a perfectly grilled octopus tentacle straight from the grill, drizzled with olive oil and a squeeze of lemon. What's more Greek than that?

FROM THE SEA

FRIED WHITEBAIT WITH
OUZO MAYONNAISE
66

OCTOPUS WITH CAPERBERRIES & LEMON
68

SARDINES WITH TOMATO & MARJORAM
71

KING PRAWNS WITH FENNEL &
CAPER BUTTER
72

SNAPPER WITH AVGOLEMONO &
CHARRED HORTA
75

BARBOUNIA TIGANITA
Fried red mullet
76

GRILLED CALAMARI WITH FAVA &
PICKLED ONION
78

TAVERNA DIARIES:
YPEROKEANIO, ATHENS -
GRILLED SARDINES & TOMATO ON
CHARRED BREAD
80

SWORDFISH WITH ROASTED GRAPES
& GREEN OLIVE SALSA
87

KAKAVIA
Fisherman's soup
88

HTAPODI ME MAKARONAKI KOFTO
Red wine octopus with small pasta
90

SCAMPI SPAGHETTI WITH CONFIT TOMATO
93

MUSSEL SAGANAKI WITH RED PEPPERS
94

PRAWN YOUVETSI
96

CLAMS WITH LEMON RICE
99

FRIED WHITEBAIT WITH OUZO MAYONNAISE

Fried whitebait is a much-loved delicacy around the Mediterranean Sea and is served at most tavernas. Fried whole in vegetable oil, these tiny fish become crispy little chips with just a light coating of flour. We would call these 'fries with eyes' when we were kids – they scared the hell out of us. They may look a little off-putting, but trust us, they are absolutely delicious.

Make sure to give the whitebait a good wash, soaking them in cold water to remove any sand. Also make sure your vegetable oil is at the right temperature for frying, as soggy whitebait is very unpleasant to eat. To test if the oil is hot enough, throw a piece of bread into the oil and watch it turn golden brown.

Feeds 4-6

vegetable oil, for deep-frying
75 g (½ cup) plain (all-purpose) flour
1 teaspoon smoked paprika, plus extra to serve
salt flakes and freshly cracked black pepper
500 g (1 lb 2 oz) whitebait
1 white onion, peeled and cut into thin wedges
lemon cheeks, to serve

OUZO MAYONNAISE
150 g (5½ oz) whole-egg mayonnaise
1 tablespoon ouzo
zest and juice of 1 small lemon

Combine all the ouzo mayonnaise ingredients in a small bowl and season to taste. Set aside until required.

Heat about 10 cm (4 in) of vegetable oil in a deep-fryer or medium-sized frying pan until the temperature comes to 180°C (350°F) on a kitchen thermometer.

Place the flour and paprika in a bowl and season with salt flakes and cracked pepper. Tossing in a few fish at a time, coat the whitebait, shaking off any excess flour, and place on a plate. Make sure not to pile them on top of each other, or they will stick together.

Add the floured whitebait to the deep-fryer in small batches and cook for 4–5 minutes, until they turn golden brown. Drain on paper towel to absorb any excess oil. Add the onion wedges to the oil and fry for 3–4 minutes, until crispy and golden.

To serve, toss the onion wedges with the whitebait and serve immediately, with lemon cheeks and the ouzo mayonnaise on the side.

A NOTE ON PREP
It's best to serve the whitebait freshly fried and straight on the table, as they will become soggy and unpleasant to eat if left to sit at room temperature.

SERVE ME WITH
For a summer feast enjoyed in the sunshine, serve the whitebait with a glass of tsipouro or beer, some Revithokeftedes (page 42), Octopus with caperberries and lemon (page 68), Horiatiki salata (page 168) - and, of course, good parea (company).

OCTOPUS WITH CAPERBERRIES & LEMON

If there is a recipe that screams summer in all its glory, it's marinated octopus. Octopus has to be one of our favourite seafoods to eat in Greece – especially when the locals are heading out in the morning to catch it fresh and serve it on the menu that same day. Here we cook our octopus in red wine vinegar, as it helps with the texture of the meat. It's worth sourcing Greek red wine vinegar if possible, you will notice the flavour is smoother than other red wine vinegars.

Don't worry, our recipe won't have you hanging your octopus.

Place the octopus in a large pot with the peppercorns, salt flakes, garlic and bay leaf. Add 2 tablespoons of the vinegar and 1 litre (4 cups) water and bring to the boil. Reduce the heat and simmer for 20 minutes, then remove the octopus from the pot and allow to cool completely.

Place the olive oil and remaining vinegar in a large non-metallic container with the lemon zest, dried oregano, and caperberries and caper leaves. Slice the cooled octopus into bite-sized pieces, then add to the marinade and mix to coat. Cover and marinate in the fridge overnight.

Remove the marinated octopus from the fridge 30 minutes before serving.

Feeds 4-6

- 1 kg (2 lb 3 oz) octopus, cleaned and gutted
- 1 tablespoon black peppercorns
- 2 teaspoons salt flakes
- 2 garlic cloves
- 1 fresh bay leaf
- 80 ml (⅓ cup) red wine vinegar
- 250 ml (1 cup) extra virgin olive oil
- peeled zest of 1 lemon
- 1 teaspoon dried Greek oregano
- 2 tablespoons caperberries and caper leaves

A NOTE ON PREP
This simple mezze is great to have in the fridge if unexpected guests arrive, as it's best served cold. Any leftover octopus can be stored in an airtight container in the fridge for up to 5 days.

SERVE ME WITH
A glass of ouzo over ice and sunshine (in Greece, if possible).

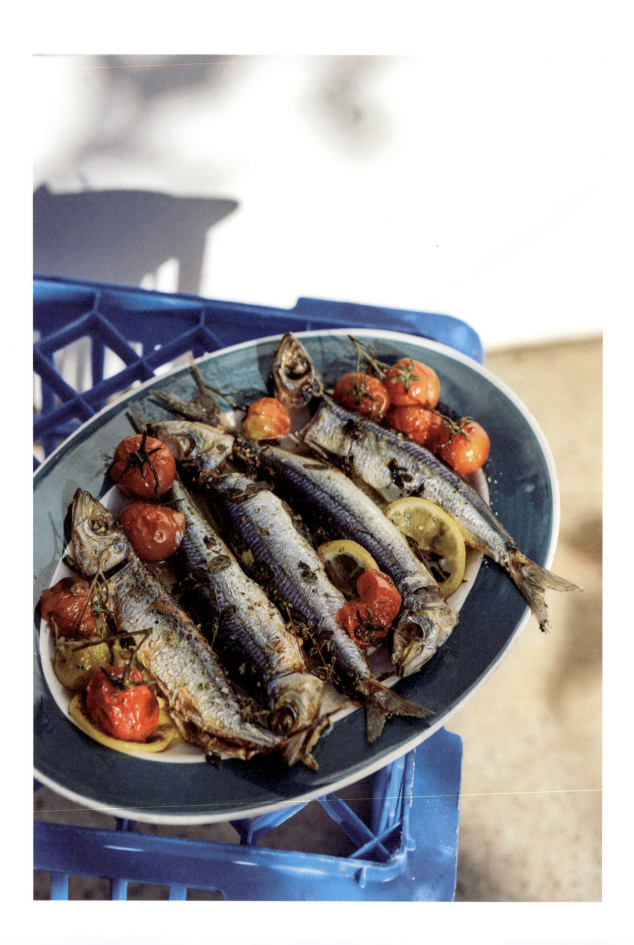

FROM THE SEA

SARDINES WITH TOMATO & MARJORAM

Whether grilled, baked or cured, sardines are so versatile. Their small size and oily texture lend them to various cooking methods, from grilling over the barbecue to roasting in the oven, as we do here. We love serving sardines at our dinner parties. We had a few friends who had never eaten them before, so our goal was to convince them to love them – and this dish did just that! Sardines have a distinct and rich flavour that pairs beautifully with sweet tomatoes and marjoram. You can use fresh oregano leaves if marjoram is not available.

Sardines vary in size; smaller ones weighing 85–100 g (3–3½ oz) are best for this recipe.

Preheat the oven to 180°C (350°F). Line a baking tray with baking paper.

Place the sardines on the baking tray in a single row. Scatter the cherry tomatoes, marjoram leaves and lemon slices around the sardines. Sprinkle with the dried oregano, season with salt flakes and drizzle with the olive oil.

Place in the oven and roast for 20 minutes, or until the sardines are just cooked. (You'll know they're cooked when the meat comes off the bone when gently pressed.)

Feeds 4

12 × 85 g (3 oz) whole sardines, scaled and gutted
500 g (1 lb 2 oz) cherry tomatoes, on the vine
¼ bunch of marjoram, leaves picked
1 large lemon, halved, then finely sliced
1 teaspoon dried Greek oregano
salt flakes
80 ml (⅓ cup) extra virgin olive oil

A NOTE ON PREP
This dish is best made fresh and served on the day of cooking. Wonderful straight from the oven, they are also lovely at room temperature.

SERVE ME WITH
For a seafood feast, serve with Fried whitebait with ouzo mayonnaise (page 66) and Patatosalata (page 174).

KING PRAWNS WITH FENNEL & CAPER BUTTER

Fresh prawns are so delicate they don't require much cooking. We first discovered this method of cooking prawns back when we were cheffing. All great recipes start with butter, and when the prawns are cooked over a barbecue, the butter browns, enhancing the sweetness of the prawns. These prawns are also delicious added to pasta – just remove the shells and roughly chop the flesh to mix through buttery cooked spaghetti, or simply enjoy with chunky bread to soak up those buttery prawn juices.

Place all the fennel and caper butter ingredients in a food processor and blitz until white and creamy, scraping down the sides of the processor a couple of times if needed. Transfer to a bowl and set aside.

Heat a greased chargrill pan or barbecue over high heat. Season the prawns with salt flakes and spread the cut side with the fennel and caper butter.

Working in batches if needed, place the prawns on the hot grill, flesh side up, so they are sitting on their shells. Grill for 4–5 minutes, adding more butter if needed, until the shells are crispy and the flesh is cooked through. Season with salt flakes. Keep warm until ready to serve. Any leftover butter can be melted in a small saucepan and drizzled over the grilled prawns to serve, alongside a squeeze of lemon juice.

Feeds 4

- 12 × 100 g (3½ oz) large raw king prawns (shrimp), split down the middle from head to tail, then deveined
- salt flakes
- lemon cheeks, to serve

FENNEL & CAPER BUTTER
- 250 g (9 oz) unsalted butter, softened
- 1 teaspoon fennel seeds, toasted
- 2 tablespoons baby capers, drained
- 1 garlic clove, crushed
- zest of 1 lemon

A NOTE ON PREP
The fennel and caper butter can be made the day before and kept in the fridge. Just bring it to room temperature a few hours before using.

SERVE ME WITH
Our favourite way to enjoy the prawns is with a Black-eyed bean salad (page 172), and a side of Patates tiganites (page 34), minus the goat's cheese.

SNAPPER WITH AVGOLEMONO & CHARRED HORTA

Our dad loved to go fishing. He owned a small boat and would quite often go out with our uncles, usually coming home with snapper or calamari. Snapper was one of his favourite fish; when cooked whole, its delicate, flaky flesh is juicy and tender. And doused with a tangy, creamy avgolemono sauce, snapper is just divine.

Avgolemono is a traditional Greek sauce made with eggs, lemon juice and stock, creating a velvety texture that complements seafood beautifully. The sauce can also be served over a roasted chicken, but try not to eat all of the sauce on its own before serving (it's so good)!

This recipe also works well with sea bass (or barramundi) if snapper isn't available.

Feeds 4

- 2 × 750 g (1 lb 11 oz) whole snapper, cleaned, gutted and scaled
- 2 lemons, finely sliced
- ½ bunch of oregano, leaves picked
- salt flakes and freshly cracked black pepper
- 80 ml (⅓ cup) olive oil
- ½ bunch of horta (wild greens), such as leaf chicory, amaranth or curly endive (frisée), washed well, leaves picked

AVGOLEMONO (LEMON SAUCE)
- 60 ml (¼ cup) lemon juice
- 1 teaspoon plain (all-purpose) flour
- 2 teaspoons cornflour (corn starch)
- 2 eggs, lightly beaten
- 250 ml (1 cup) fish stock
- pinch of ground white pepper

For the avgolemono sauce, whisk the lemon juice, flour, cornflour and egg in a bowl for about 5 minutes, until frothy. Pour the mixture into a small saucepan, along with the fish stock, and whisk continuously over medium-low heat for about 6 minutes, until the sauce has thickened. Season with white pepper. Keep the sauce warm by placing a lid over the pan; if the sauce cools down, gently warm it over low heat for serving.

Preheat the oven to 200°C (400°F). Grease a large baking tray and line with baking paper. Place the fish on the tray and stuff the cavities with the lemon slices and oregano leaves. Season with salt flakes and cracked pepper and drizzle with half the olive oil. Roast for 25–30 minutes, until the fish is flaky and cooked through.

Heat the remaining olive oil in a large frying pan over medium-high heat and fry the horta for 4–5 minutes, until lightly charred.

Arrange the snapper on a large serving platter, along with the horta. Drizzle the avgolemono sauce over the fish.

A NOTE ON PREP
The sauce can be made the day before and gently reheated when ready to serve; if the sauce is too thick, stir in a dash of fish stock to loosen it slightly. The fish is best cooked fresh and served immediately.

SERVE ME WITH
For a fresh seafood feast, serve alongside Tuna with blood orange and shallot vinaigrette (page 28), King prawns with fennel & caper butter (page 72), and, for some freshness, our Maroulosalata (page 171).

BARBOUNIA TIGANITA
Fried red mullet

Barbounia is a favourite fish among the coastal tavernas. We don't eat much red mullet here in Australia, but it's a dish we order the second we arrive at a seafood taverna.

It's really important to use olive oil for frying here, as it enhances the flavour and richness of the fish.

Combine the flour, cornflour, paprika, cumin and cracked pepper in a bowl and season with salt flakes.

Heat 1 cm (½ in) olive oil in a large frying pan over medium heat. Lightly dust the fish with the flour mixture, shaking off any excess flour.

Working in batches, add the fish to the pan and fry for 5–6 minutes on each side, until golden brown and crispy. Transfer to a plate lined with paper towel to absorb any excess oil.

Serve hot, with lemon wedges.

Feeds 4

- 35 g (¼ cup) plain (all-purpose) flour
- 1 tablespoon cornflour (corn starch)
- 1 teaspoon smoked paprika
- ½ teaspoon ground cumin
- ½ teaspoon freshly cracked black pepper
- salt flakes
- olive oil, for shallow-frying
- 8 small whole red mullet, scaled and gutted
- lemon wedges, to serve

A NOTE ON PREP
Get your fishmonger to scale and gut your fish for you. The fish needs to be fried just before serving.

SERVE ME WITH
At a taverna, we love ordering barbounia with horta (wild greens), to eat as we sip on an ouzo while listening to the cicadas.

GRILLED CALAMARI WITH FAVA & PICKLED ONION

Our cousin Con-Ross has been catching squid since he was a little boy, and calamari reminds us of him. Usually he will clean and gut the freshly caught squid on the boat, or, failing that, the second he gets home. He slices it into rings, then tosses it into some seasoned flour and straight into a hot pot of oil – seriously incredible. It's crucial to get the cooking time correct, as no one likes rubbery, chewy calamari.

'Fava' – one of the most famous recipes to come from the Greek island of Santorini – isn't actually made with fava (broad) beans, but yellow split peas. The creamy fava with the grilled calamari is summer on a plate… and we promise this will be your go-to dish to serve up when the days are long and warm.

Use a sharp knife to deeply score the body of each calamari with a series of incisions – but don't cut all the way through, you still want to keep the body whole. Place in a bowl with the dried oregano and half the olive oil, coating the squid well.

In a separate bowl, combine the red onion and lemon juice and season with salt flakes. Set aside to pickle for 30 minutes.

To make the fava, heat the olive oil in a saucepan over medium heat and cook the onion and garlic, stirring occasionally, for 8–10 minutes, until the onion has softened. Add the split peas and cook, stirring constantly, for another 4–5 minutes, until slightly toasted. Pour in the stock, add the bay leaf and cook for a further 50–55 minutes, until the peas are tender and have broken down. Skim off any foam that rises to the surface during the cooking time. Discard the bay leaf and, using a stick blender, blitz until smooth and creamy.

Heat a barbecue or chargrill pan over high heat. Grill the calamari on both sides for 4–5 minutes, until charred and cooked through. Add the lemon halves, cut side down, to the grill and cook for 3–5 minutes, until charred and jammy.

Add the basil leaves to the pickled red onion mixture, along with the remaining olive oil, and mix to combine.

To serve, spread the fava onto a serving platter, then top with the grilled calamari, pickled onion mixture, caperberries and a good squeeze of the grilled lemon.

Feeds 4

- 2 × 1 kg (2 lb 3 oz) whole calamari, cleaned and gutted, tentacles attached
- 1 tablespoon dried Greek oregano
- 80 ml (⅓ cup) olive oil
- 1 small red onion, finely chopped
- 2 tablespoons lemon juice, plus 1 lemon, halved
- salt flakes
- small handful of basil leaves, finely chopped
- 2 tablespoons caperberries, drained

FAVA
- 2 tablespoons olive oil
- 1 brown onion, chopped
- 2 garlic cloves, sliced
- 300 g (10½ oz) yellow split peas, washed well
- 750 ml (3 cups) vegetable stock
- 1 fresh or dried bay leaf

A NOTE ON PREP
The fava can be made the day before – simply cool it completely, then store in an airtight container in the fridge. When ready to serve, place the cold fava in a small saucepan over low heat and stir in 1–2 tablespoons vegetable stock or water to loosen it slightly. Warm through for about 10 minutes, until the fava is smooth.

SERVE ME WITH
When we order calamari at a taverna, we love having it with horta (wild greens). This will also pair beautifully with our Rice-stuffed zucchini flowers (page 133).

Set in the heart of Piraeus, the chief sea port of Athens, is YPEROKEANIO, a mesmerising fish taverna that transports you back in time with its 1950s decor, traditional dishes and vintage memorabilia. The taverna takes its name from the first ocean liners - yperokeania - that departed from this port over a century ago, loaded with Greek immigrants bound for the United States and Australia.

Yperokeanio was founded fifteen years ago by Andreas L Kantsos, whose family grew up on the island of Kimolos in the Cyclades. The sea had always been a big part of Andreas' life, due to his heritage and his job as a sea captain. So when family matters drew him back to shore, he decided to open a fish taverna as a way of paying tribute to the culinary traditions of the Greek islands - hence the nostalgic retro decor.

The menu at Yperokeanio is very traditional and strongly inspired by the island of Kimolos, transporting you to a beach sipping tsipouro (a Greek distilled spirit) or ouzo with good friends and eating fresh, traditional mezedes such as sardines, dolmades, eggplant (aubergine) salad and fried zucchini (courgette) - all ideal for pairing with tsipouro. Andreas takes pride in sourcing ingredients carefully. The bread comes from an old bakery in Evia, the olive oil from Mani in Messinia, and the seafood is bought fresh every day from the fish market. The dishes are simple yet thoughtful, designed to offer a unique and memorable taste - such as the sardine bruschetta, a recipe inspired by the fishermen of Kimolos, featuring lightly grilled sardines with lemon, oregano and olive oil served with freshly sliced tomatoes on perfectly charred bread. Simple and yet so tasty.

The backbone of this taverna is Ilona, a woman who has exceptional cooking skills and a talent for creating dishes that transport you to a Greek island. Although not a cook himself, Andreas has a very good palette and knows exactly how a dish should taste. Together they bring out the best in every dish and deliver it to their guests with a warm smile.

"Yperokeanio is dedicated to preserving traditions, even as the taverna life and culture in Greece evolves"

People travel from all parts of Athens to visit this celebrated taverna all year round. During winter, a hearty bouillabaisse-style fish soup keeps guests warm and makes them feel right at home. In summer, diners get the chance to sample the traditional baked flatbread with garlic, oregano, tomato and onion - a unique dish that is usually found only on the island of Kimolos. We also ordered the fried calamari, which was fresh and tender, dusted with flour and semolina, and seasoned with only salt flakes and a good squeeze of lemon juice. This really is summer on a plate.

Yperokeanio is dedicated to preserving traditions, even as the taverna life and culture in Greece evolves. Andreas is passionate about providing guests with a genuine culinary experience that truly reflects Greece's rich food culture.

One of the joys of writing a cookbook is discovering places like Yperokeanio, where the love for seafood is so strong. We knew we had to share their most ordered dish with you. It's incredibly simple, yet the flavours come together beautifully.

GRILLED SARDINES & TOMATO ON CHARRED BREAD

Feeds 4 as a starter

- 3 thin slices wholemeal (wholewheat) sourdough bread, cut in half
- 60 ml (¼ cup) extra virgin olive oil
- 2 teaspoons lemon juice
- 1 teaspoon dried Greek oregano
- salt flakes and freshly cracked black pepper
- 10 fresh sardines, gutted and butterflied, bones removed
- 1 large tomato, sliced
- 1 red onion, diced

Drizzle the bread with 1 tablespoon of the olive oil.

In a small bowl, whisk together the remaining oil, lemon juice and oregano and season with salt flakes and cracked pepper. Place the sardines on a plate and brush them all over with the marinade mixture, reserving the remaining marinade for serving.

Heat a barbecue or chargrill pan over medium–high heat. Add the sardines, skin side down, and grill for 2–4 minutes on each side, until cooked through and lightly charred. Remove from the grill and keep warm.

Toast the bread slices on the barbecue or chargrill pan for 1–2 minutes on each side, until lightly charred.

Lay the toasted sourdough slices on a serving dish and top with the sliced tomato, grilled sardines and onion. Drizzle with the remaining marinade mixture and serve hot.

A NOTE ON PREP
To save time, get your fishmonger to butterfly and gut the sardines for you.

SERVE ME WITH
A glass of assyrtiko, Greece's most famous white wine variety.

Swordfish with Roasted Grapes & Green Olive Salsa

In our family, cooking fish isn't just about preparing a meal, it's a way of honouring our dad's deep love for fishing. Growing up, we always had our boat in the driveway, a constant reminder of the countless hours Dad spent out on the water, competing in fishing tournaments and creating memories that became stories shared around the dinner table. Whenever we cook fish now, it's like Dad is right there with us – and we remember how he would have prepared each fillet (shirtless in the backyard).

For this particular dish, we have added the grapes as our little touch. We think Dad would have thought the grapes were a crazy addition, yet the sweetness from the roasted grapes and the tang from the green olive salsa are lovely with the swordfish. These roasted grapes are also great to add to a cheese board.

Preheat the oven to 200°C (400°F). Line a baking tray with baking paper.

Place the white grapes on the baking tray and drizzle with the honey and 1 tablespoon of the olive oil. Season lightly with salt flakes. Bake for 20 minutes, or until the grapes are lightly roasted but are still holding their shape.

Meanwhile, place all the green olive salsa ingredients in a bowl and mix to combine. Set aside for serving.

Heat a large chargrill or griddle pan over medium–high heat. Drizzle the swordfish fillets with the remaining olive oil and season with salt flakes on both sides. Fry the swordfish for 2–3 minutes on each side, until lightly charred and cooked through.

Divide the swordfish among serving plates, along with the roasted grapes and fresh grapes, then drizzle the green olive salsa over.

Feeds 4

- 300 g (10½ oz) white grapes, on the vine
- 2 teaspoons honey
- 60 ml (¼ cup) olive oil
- salt flakes
- 4 × 200 g (7 oz) swordfish fillets, skin off, bones removed
- 100 g (3½ oz) small purple grapes, halved

GREEN OLIVE SALSA

- 150 g (5½ oz) green olives, pitted and chopped
- 60 ml (¼ cup) extra virgin olive oil
- 2 teaspoons white wine vinegar
- 1 tablespoon fresh oregano leaves, chopped

A NOTE ON PREP
The green olive salsa can be prepared the day before; just add the oregano leaves when you are ready to serve. The grapes can also be roasted the day before and stored at room temperature, then gently reheated in a low oven for a few minutes to warm through slightly. The swordfish is best cooked just before serving.

SERVE ME WITH
Patates lemonates (page 180) and a Ouzo and olive oil sour (page 236) – followed by our Sour cherry and vermouth granita (page 215) for dessert.

KAKAVIA
Fisherman's soup

Kakavia is a traditional Greek fisherman's soup, often made with a variety of seafood, potatoes and tomatoes and cooked in a rich broth. The soup takes its name after a 'kakavi' – a large tripod cooking pot the fishermen would have on their boats. Any seafood they caught that was too small to sell at the markets would go straight into the pot and be cooked over an open fire on board the boat.

We love using blue-eye cod and mussels in this soup, but feel free to use prawns (shrimp) and any kind of firm white fish, such as snapper or red mullet. We've also added fennel here, which adds a little sweetness to the soup.

Feeds 4-6

- 60 ml (¼ cup) olive oil, plus extra for drizzling
- 1 white onion, finely chopped
- 2 garlic cloves, crushed
- 1 fennel bulb, finely sliced
- ½ teaspoon fennel seeds
- salt flakes
- 1 carrot, cut into 2 cm (¾ in) rounds
- 400 g (14 oz) chat (baby) potatoes, peeled and halved
- 1.25 litres (5 cups) vegetable stock
- 2 large tomatoes, roughly chopped
- 1 × 600 g (1 lb 5 oz) blue-eye cod, skin and bones removed, flesh cut into 5 cm (2 in) chunks
- 20 mussels, scrubbed well, beards removed

Heat the olive oil in a large deep saucepan over medium–low heat. Add the onion, garlic, fennel and fennel seeds and season with salt flakes. Cook, stirring occasionally, for 10–12 minutes, until the vegetables are soft.

Add the carrot and potatoes and cook for 2–4 minutes, then add the stock and tomatoes and simmer over medium heat for a further 20–25 minutes, until the vegetables are tender.

Add the fish and mussels, then cover and cook for a final 10 minutes or so, until the fish is cooked through and the mussels have opened. Discard any mussels that haven't opened.

Drizzle with extra olive oil to serve.

A NOTE ON PREP
This soup is best made just before serving, as you don't want to overcook the seafood. If time is short, make the soup broth the day before, minus the fish and mussels – then the following day, when ready to serve, gently reheat the soup, add the seafood and simmer until the fish and mussels are cooked through.

SERVE ME WITH
When ready to serve, squeeze some lemon over and scatter with chopped dill. Soak up the broth with Pita bread with confit garlic oil (page 26), or our Horiatiko psomi (page 59).

HTAPODI ME MAKARONAKI KOFTO
Red wine octopus with small pasta

The popular small, short pasta called 'kofto' is usually enjoyed during Lent before Easter – which is when you're likely to find it on a menu. And in the warmer months, you'll often find it paired with octopus slowly braised in a red wine sauce. You might also notice freshly caught octopus hanging outside coastal tavernas. Fishermen commonly tenderise the octopus by beating it against rocks, a time-honoured technique that enhances its flavour and texture.

Heat the olive oil in a large saucepan over medium–high heat. Add the onion and cook, stirring occasionally, for 8–9 minutes, until the onion has softened.

Add the garlic, octopus, oregano, thyme sprigs, cumin and paprika and cook, stirring occasionally, for about 5 minutes, until the octopus changes colour. Pour in the red wine and simmer for about 3 minutes, until reduced by half.

Stir in the tomato paste, cherry tomatoes and 60 ml (¼ cup) water, then bring to a simmer. Reduce the heat to low, cover with a lid and simmer for 1–1¼ hours, until the octopus is tender.

Just before serving, cook the pasta in a large saucepan of boiling salted water, following the packet instructions. Drain.

Divide the pasta among serving bowls and top with the octopus, red wine sauce and extra thyme leaves.

Feeds 4

- 60 ml (¼ cup) extra virgin olive oil
- 1 white onion, finely chopped
- 2 garlic cloves, sliced
- 1 kg (2 lb 3 oz) baby octopus, cleaned and gutted, tentacles cut in half
- 1 teaspoon dried Greek oregano
- 2 lemon thyme sprigs, plus extra leaves to serve
- 1 teaspoon ground cumin
- 1 teaspoon sweet paprika
- 400 ml (13½ fl oz) red wine
- 2 tablespoons tomato paste (concentrated puree)
- 800 g (1 lb 12 oz) tinned cherry tomatoes
- 500 g (1 lb 2 oz) short pasta, such as ditali

A NOTE ON PREP
The octopus can be simmered the day before; allow to cool completely before storing in the fridge. The flavours will develop overnight. If the octopus isn't saucy enough, just add a splash of water when reheating it for serving.

SERVE ME WITH
If you're having a few people over, serve this with our Ouzo and olive oil sours (page 236), Tuna with blood orange and shallot vinaigrette (page 28) and Beetroot with mizithra cheese (page 177).

SCAMPI SPAGHETTI WITH CONFIT TOMATO

In the summer of 2024, when Helena visited the beautiful island of Naxos in the Cyclades, we headed to a restaurant right in front of the beach that a local had recommended to us. We love how simple the Greeks like to keep dishes, allowing the produce to speak for itself. The pasta we ordered was tossed in a delicious light sauce made from confit tomatoes, the slow-cooking released all the beautiful juices from those luscious summer tomatoes.

Scampi is a delicacy in fish tavernas, usually served raw as an appetiser. Here, the sweetness of the scampi and confit tomato complement each other perfectly. If you can't find scampi you can use king prawns (shrimp) instead.

Feeds 4

- 60 ml (¼ cup) olive oil
- 2 tablespoons unsalted butter
- 3 garlic cloves, sliced
- 350 g (12½ oz) mixed cherry tomatoes
- 2 tablespoons finely chopped parsley stalks, plus a small handful of parsley leaves, chopped
- 1 long red chilli, sliced (optional)
- 400 g (14 oz) spaghetti
- 16 raw scampi, heads removed
- freshly cracked black pepper

Place a large saucepan over low heat. Add the olive oil, butter, garlic, tomatoes, parsley stalks and chilli, if using. Gently cook for 30 minutes, until the tomatoes have softened and are slightly caramelised, stirring occasionally.

Cook the spaghetti in a large saucepan of boiling salted water, following the packet instructions.

While the spaghetti is cooking, add the scampi to the confit tomato mixture, increase the heat to medium and simmer for 5 minutes, or until the scampi are cooked and turn white.

Drain the spaghetti, reserving 60 ml (¼ cup) of the pasta water. Add the spaghetti to the confit tomato mixture, along with the reserved pasta water. Toss to combine, then divide among serving plates. Scatter with the parsley leaves and cracked pepper.

A NOTE ON PREP
The confit tomato can be made the day before and stored at room temperature in an airtight container.

SERVE ME WITH
Horiatiki salata (page 168). For a refreshing finish, serve the Ouzo and citrus sorbet (page 216) for dessert.

Mussel Saganaki with Red Peppers

Mussel or prawn saganaki is a classic dish offered by seafood tavernas. The word 'saganaki', meaning 'little frying pan', refers to both the pan the dish is cooked in and the way the dish has been cooked. Usually mussel or prawn saganaki is cooked in a saganaki pan, with a rich pepper and tomato salsa and scattered with feta.

You may be more familiar with fried saganaki, where kefalotyri or kasseri cheese is dusted in flour and pan-fried, traditionally in a saganaki pan. It's the one dish we tend to order again and again – but maybe this one will become your new favourite.

Feel free to use prawns (shrimp) instead of mussels here; simply cook them for 10–12 minutes.

Heat the olive oil in a large ovenproof saucepan over medium heat and fry the onion, red pepper and garlic for 8–10 minutes, until softened. Add the oregano and tomato paste and cook for a further 2 minutes, or until caramelised. Stir in the wine and allow the wine to reduce by half. Add the cherry tomatoes and 80 ml (⅓ cup) water and simmer for 15 minutes, or until the liquid has thickened.

Preheat the oven grill to 250°C (480°F).

Increase the stovetop heat to medium–high. Arrange the mussels in the pan over the sauce, then cover with a lid and cook, shaking the pan constantly, for 10–12 minutes, until the mussels have opened. Discard any mussels that don't open; these are not safe to eat.

Remove the lid from the saucepan. Crumble the feta over the mussels, then place the pan in the hot oven for 5–8 minutes, until the feta is lightly golden. Drizzle with a little extra olive oil and serve with lemon wedges.

Feeds 4

- 2 tablespoons extra virgin olive oil, plus extra for drizzling
- 1 brown onion, chopped
- 1 red pepper (capsicum), chopped
- 2 garlic cloves, crushed
- 1 tablespoon fresh oregano leaves, finely chopped
- 1 tablespoon tomato paste (concentrated puree)
- 80 ml (⅓ cup) white wine
- 400 g (14 oz) tinned cherry tomatoes
- 500 g (1 lb 2 oz) mussels, scrubbed well, beards removed
- 70 g (2½ oz) Greek feta
- lemon wedges, to serve

A NOTE ON PREP
The tomato-based sauce can be made the day before and reheated just before the mussels go in. The mussels need to be added fresh on the day of serving.

SERVE ME WITH
Charred bread, and Beetroot with mizithra cheese (page 177).

PRAWN YOUVETSI

Prawn youvetsi is served at most good seafood tavernas across the Greek islands. Originally, youvetsi was typically made with lamb or beef, and cooked in a tomato-based sauce. The word 'youvetsi' refers to the Greek clay pot in which the dish is traditionally cooked, which gives a distinctive flavour and texture. Our version is simmered on the stovetop.

Making a prawn stock using the shells and heads is a great way to extract maximum flavour from the prawns. To save on time, double the quantity of prawn stock and freeze half for next time – your future self will thank you.

For the prawn stock, heat the olive oil in a large saucepan over high heat. Add the reserved prawn heads and shells and cook, stirring occasionally, for about 5 minutes, until the shells start to colour. Add the onion, garlic, fennel, bay leaf and peppercorns and cook, stirring now and then, for 6–8 minutes, until the vegetables have softened.

Stir in the tomato paste and cook, stirring, for 2 minutes. Pour in 1.25 litres (5 cups) boiling water. Reduce the heat to low and simmer for 20–25 minutes, skimming occasionally, until the stock has reduced to about 1 litre (4 cups). Strain through a fine-meshed sieve and discard the solids; set aside and keep the stock warm. You should have about 850 ml (28½ fl oz) of stock.

Heat the olive oil in a large saucepan over medium heat. Fry the onion for 8–9 minutes, until softened, then add the garlic and oregano and cook for a further 3 minutes. Add the tomato paste and risoni and cook, stirring, for 2 minutes, or until the risoni grains are completely coated.

Pour in the prawn stock and bring to a simmer. Reduce the heat to medium-low and simmer, stirring occasionally, for 10–15 minutes, until the risoni is cooked, stirring in the prawns for the last 5 minutes of cooking. Add the lemon juice and season to taste.

Scatter the prawn youvetsi with the lemon zest and reserved fennel fronds. Serve immediately.

Feeds 4

2 tablespoons olive oil
1 white onion, finely chopped
2 garlic cloves, crushed
small handful of oregano leaves, chopped
2 teaspoons tomato paste (concentrated puree)
300 g (10½ oz) dried risoni
zest and juice of 1 lemon
salt flakes and freshly cracked black pepper

PRAWN STOCK
1 tablespoon olive oil
20 large raw king prawns (shrimp), peeled, tails intact, heads and shells reserved
1 brown onion, roughly chopped
2 garlic cloves, crushed
1 fennel bulb, roughly chopped, fronds reserved for serving
1 fresh or dried bay leaf
1 teaspoon whole black peppercorns
2 teaspoons tomato paste (concentrated puree)

A NOTE ON PREP
The stock can be made the day before and stored in the fridge. Save time and have your fishmonger clean the prawns for you – just don't forget to take the heads and shells with you!

SERVE ME WITH
A glass of rose or assyrtiko wine and a Dakos salad (page 178).

CLAMS WITH LEMON RICE

It was on a holiday to the island of Skopelos that we first ate clams with rice. It was a warm summer's afternoon, we were sitting with friends. The rice was lemony, spiked with fresh dill, the clams were the freshest ones we had ever eaten, and we remember thinking we just had to share this recipe in our next book. The best part is when the rice sticks to the clams, and you get to suck all the delicious juices from the shells.

Mussels are a great substitute here if you prefer them to clams.

Heat the olive oil and butter in a large saucepan over medium heat. Add the onion and cook, stirring occasionally, for 7–8 minutes, until the onion has softened. Stir in the garlic, rice and half the lemon zest and cook for about 2 minutes, until the rice is coated. Pour in the wine and cook for about 5 minutes, until reduced by half.

Add the clams and stock, cover with a lid and cook for about 30 minutes, until the rice is tender and the clams have opened. Discard any unopened clams.

Pour in the lemon juice and carefully stir it through. Scatter with the dill and remaining lemon zest, finish with a drizzle of olive oil and serve immediately.

Feeds 4

- 2 tablespoons extra virgin olive oil, plus extra to serve
- 1 tablespoon salted butter
- 1 white onion, finely sliced
- 2 garlic cloves, crushed
- 300 g (1½ cups) medium-grain white rice, rinsed
- zest of 2 small lemons, plus 60 ml (¼ cup) lemon juice
- 125 ml (½ cup) white wine
- 1 kg (2 lb 3 oz) small clams, purged
- 625 ml (2½ cups) vegetable stock
- small handful of dill leaves, chopped

A NOTE ON PREP
This dish is best enjoyed the day it's made. It's worth making a pit stop at your local fish market to purchase the clams.

SERVE ME WITH
A glass of assyrtiko white wine and a Black-eyed bean salad (page 172). It's also lovely served with Tuna with blood orange and shallot vinaigrette (page 28) as a starter.

MEAT

ΚΡΕΑΣ ΤΗΣ ΩΡΑΣ

On almost every taverna menu, you'll stumble upon a section labelled 'Tis Oras', listing a selection of cooked-to-order grilled meats.

Imagine sinking your teeth into succulent Biftekia (page 114), a juicy pork steak or tender psaronefri (pork tenderloin fillet), each grilled to mouthwatering perfection, glistening with a mix of salt and oregano, and typically served with a side of crispy, golden Patates tiganites (page 34). If you're fortunate enough to find a local taverna cooking lamb chops (paidakia) over charcoal, you're in for a treat.

Another beloved dish, commonly known as souvlaki, or kalamaki (depending on where you are in Greece), consists of cubes of meat threaded onto skewers and cooked over charcoal. In Greece, pork is the preferred meat, while in our native Australia, lamb and chicken are firm favourites. The meat is marinated in a blend of garlic, lemon juice and olive oil, bringing out those classic Greek flavours we all love.

In Greece, many cultural traditions centre around communally sharing meat dishes. One such tradition is Tsiknopempti, translating to 'Charred Thursday'. This day, observed 11 days before Clean Monday (the onset of the 40-day Lent period in the Orthodox calendar), sees every neighbourhood and village filled with smoky wafts as meat is grilled from morning until evening to celebrate. It doesn't matter if you are gathering at home, at a taverna, or even if you are working (many local businesses will grill something for workers while they work), every meat-eating Greek will participate in this day.

MEAT

CHICKEN SOUVLAKI WITH
GREEK FRIES
106

PORK CHOPS WITH ROASTED
PEPPER BUTTER
108

LOUKANIKO WITH WHITE
ONION & CUCUMBERS
111

PORK SPARE RIBS WITH
LEMON & OREGANO
112

BIFTEKIA WITH TZATZIKI
114

LAMB CHOPS WITH PICKLED
PEPPER & SHALLOT
117

HONEY CHICKEN WINGS WITH GALOTYRI
& GREEN PEPPER HERBY OIL
118

GRILLED LAMB'S LIVER WITH ONIONS
120

TAVERNA DIARIES:
TAVERNA KRONOS, THESSALONIKI -
SOUTZOUKAKIA ON THE GRILL
122

CHICKEN SOUVLAKI WITH GREEK FRIES

Souvlaki is one of Greece's most popular street foods, and our favourite to eat all year round. Traditionally pork is used, and sometimes chicken, lamb or beef.

If you're wondering about the difference between a souvlaki and a gyros, a souvlaki ('meat on a skewer') is made by threading pieces of marinated meat onto a skewer and grilling it over charcoal for added flavour. A traditional gyros usually uses pork, and is cooked on a vertical rotisserie; it's then shaved and added to a warm pita bread spread with tzatziki and topped with slices of tomato, finely sliced onion, fresh parsley and fried potatoes.

Our souvlaki recipe uses chicken thighs, marinated in the classic Greek marinade for most meats – freshly squeezed lemon juice, crushed garlic, dried Greek oregano, olive oil, and a good seasoning of salt and pepper. Avoid using chicken breast for these skewers, as the meat becomes too dry on the grill.

You will need six metal skewers for this recipe; if using wooden skewers, soak them in water for 1 hour before cooking, so they don't burn.

In a bowl, combine the garlic, lemon zest and juice, oregano and olive oil and season with salt flakes and cracked pepper. Add the chicken and toss to coat. Cover and leave to marinate in the fridge for at least 1 hour, or overnight.

Preheat a barbecue or chargrill pan over medium–high heat. Thread 5–6 chicken pieces onto each skewer. Grill the chicken, turning frequently, for 15 minutes, or until golden brown and cooked through.

Serve the warm skewers with tzatziki and Greek fries.

Feeds 4

4 garlic cloves, crushed
zest and juice of 1 small lemon
1 teaspoon dried Greek oregano
60 ml (¼ cup) olive oil
salt flakes and freshly cracked black pepper
1 kg (2 lb 3 oz) boneless, skinless chicken thighs, cut into 4 cm (1½ in) chunks
Tzatziki (page 114), to serve
Greek fries (page 34, made without the feta topping), to serve

A NOTE ON PREP
Marinate the chicken the day before grilling to help the flavour develop. On the morning of your gathering, pull the chicken from the fridge and thread it onto your skewers, ready for cooking.

SERVE ME WITH
A cold bottle of Greek beer. The souvlaki can also be turned into a gyros: remove the meat from the skewer and pile into a warm pita bread layered with Tirokafteri (page 20), some sliced tomato and onion, and Greek fries.

PORK CHOPS WITH ROASTED PEPPER BUTTER

Pork has been a Greek staple for centuries. Souvlaki (grilled pork skewers), gyros (seasoned pork cooked on a vertical rotisserie and served sliced in a pita wrap with sauces), kokkinisto (a braised pork stew with tomatoes, onions, garlic and spices), loukaniko (Greek pork sausage) and pastourma (a spiced, cured pork loin, similar to a dry-cured ham) are all popular Greek classics.

These chargrilled pork chops are the essence of simplicity, topped with a savoury roasted pepper butter that you'll want on absolutely everything.

Place all the roasted pepper butter ingredients in a food processor. Season with salt flakes and cracked pepper. Blend for 4–5 minutes, until the butter is creamy, scraping down the sides of the processor as needed.

Place a large piece of plastic wrap on your work surface. Spoon the butter mixture into the centre and carefully roll in to a sausage shape, twisting the ends to seal. Place the butter in the fridge for 4–6 hours, until hardened.

Season the pork cutlets with the paprika and season with salt flakes and cracked pepper.

Heat a lightly greased barbecue or chargrill pan over medium-high heat. Grill the pork cutlets for 3–4 minutes on each side, until charred and cooked through. Allow the pork to rest for 5–6 minutes before serving.

To serve, cut the butter into 1 cm (½ in) slices and place on top of the pork cutlets, allowing the butter to melt.

Feeds 4

salt flakes and freshly cracked black pepper
4 × 300 g (10½ oz) pork loin cutlets, each about 1 cm (½ in) thick
1 teaspoon smoked paprika

ROASTED PEPPER BUTTER
250 g (9 oz) unsalted butter, softened
150 g (5½ oz) jarred roasted peppers (capsicums), drained and chopped
zest of 1 lemon
1 teaspoon smoked paprika
1 teaspoon dijon mustard

A NOTE ON PREP
The roasted pepper butter can be made the day before, and any leftover butter will keep in the fridge for up to 2 weeks.

SERVE ME WITH
Beetroot with mizithra cheese (page 177) and a glass of assyrtiko white wine.

MEAT

LOUKANIKO WITH WHITE ONION & CUCUMBERS

This recipe is inspired by a restaurant in Amorgos called Kath'Odon, where they serve the most delicious loukaniko. A popular mezze among the Greeks, loukaniko is a flavoursome sausage made in most villages using local meat – either cured pork or lamb – that has been spiked with garlic, spices, dried herbs and red wine. Cooking them on the barbecue adds an extra depth of flavour. You can often find the sausages at European delicatessens, or a good local butcher.

Serve some grilled loukaniko for your guests while the rest of the food is cooking, as it really is a great appetiser to start on. Perfect with a glass of tsipouro.

Heat a chargrill pan or barbecue over high heat. Cook the loukaniko for 3–4 minutes, turning now and then, until charred.

Slice the loukaniko into bite-sized pieces and serve with the onion, cucumber slices, caperberries and lemon wedges.

Feeds 4

```
4 loukaniko
1 white onion, sliced into
    rounds
1 short cucumber, finely sliced
caperberries and lemon wedges,
    to serve
```

SERVE ME WITH
A Dakos salad (page 178) and Pita breads with confit garlic oil (page 26).

PORK SPARE RIBS WITH LEMON & OREGANO

During winter, the city of Thessaloniki becomes lively with festive barbecues and street parties. Our friend Yihao throws the best psistaria (barbecue) gathering in front of his family's Chinese restaurant, Huang, which is one of the best in Thessaloniki. Yihao always cooks the best pork spare ribs on the barbecue and is an absolute master. His mum will make a couple of salads, and everyone else will bring something sweet.

Feeds 4-6

1 bunch of oregano
salt flakes and freshly cracked black pepper
1 kg (2 lb 3 oz) pork spare ribs (bone-in pork belly), cut into 1.5 cm (½ in) thick slices
lemon wedges, to serve

LEMON & OREGANO OIL
125 ml (½ cup) olive oil
zest of 1 lemon, plus extra to serve
1 tablespoon dried Greek oregano

Tie the oregano bunch together using kitchen twine to use as your basting brush.

In a bowl, combine all the lemon and oregano oil ingredients and season with salt flakes and cracked pepper.

Season the pork spare ribs with salt flakes and cracked pepper.

Heat a chargrill pan or barbecue over high heat. Grill the pork for 5–6 minutes on each side, until the pork is charred and cooked through, basting every minute with the lemon and oregano oil, using the bunch of oregano as your brush.

Remove the pork from the grill, cover with foil and allow to rest for 5–10 minutes. Serve with a good squeeze of fresh lemon juice.

A NOTE ON PREP
Ask your butcher to slice the spare ribs for you. To enhance the flavour, you can marinate the pork overnight in the lemon and oregano oil, then brush with a fresh batch of lemon and oregano oil during grilling.

The oil can also be made the day before and stored at room temperature in a sealed jar.

SERVE ME WITH
Patatosalata (page 174) and Melitzanosalata (page 25).

BIFTEKIA WITH TZATZIKI

Greeks cherish their barbecue. Most homes will have one that's been handed down from a papou (grandpa). We remember attending our cousin's gatherings, usually on a Sunday, and of course Dad and our uncles would congregate around the barbecue, making sure the meat was cooked to perfection, like it was their one mission in life. It's a sight we miss, to be honest.

Biftekia are the Greek version of a burger patty and are either chargrilled or baked in the oven. When purchasing your minced meat, make sure not to use lean mince as the biftekia will become dry; they need the fat to remain juicy.

Adding grated tomato to the meat mixture helps give the biftekia a fluffy interior, and the red wine can be substituted with water.

To make the tzatziki, grate the cucumbers and squeeze to remove any excess liquid. Place in a large bowl with the remaining tzatziki ingredients and season with salt flakes and cracked pepper.

In a large bowl, combine all the bifteki ingredients. Shape the mixture into 10 patties, using about 125 g (4½ oz) of the mixture for each, then flatten slightly. Season with salt flakes.

Heat a chargrill pan or barbecue over medium–high heat. Working in batches, if needed, cook the patties for 5 minutes on each side, or until lightly charred and cooked through.

Feeds 4-6

salt flakes

BIFTEKIA (MAKES 10)
- 425 g (15 oz) minced (ground) beef
- 425 g (15 oz) minced (ground) pork
- 1 large egg, lightly beaten
- 1 red onion, grated and squeezed to remove any excess liquid
- 1 large tomato, grated, skin discarded
- 2 garlic cloves, crushed
- small handful of parsley, finely chopped
- 1 teaspoon dried mint
- 1 teaspoon dried Greek oregano
- 50 g (1¾ oz) fresh breadcrumbs
- 2 tablespoons red wine or water

TZATZIKI (MAKES 2 CUPS)
- 250 g (9 oz) or 2 short cucumbers, peeled
- 300 g (10½ oz) Greek-style yoghurt, strained overnight (see introduction, page 20)
- 1 garlic clove, crushed
- small handful of mint leaves, finely chopped
- small handful of dill leaves, finely chopped
- 2 tablespoons lemon juice
- 2 teaspoons extra virgin olive oil

A NOTE ON PREP
The bifteki mixture can be made the day before and left covered overnight in the fridge. The tzatziki can also be made a day ahead - in fact, we love to make it in advance as it helps the flavour develop.

SERVE ME WITH
Patates lemonates (page 180) and a Greek beer! Or, you can turn the patties into a burger: toast a burger bun and spread both cut sides with tzatziki, then fill with a bifteki patty, some sliced tomato and red onion, cos (romaine) lettuce and a slice of feta.

LAMB CHOPS WITH PICKLED PEPPER & SHALLOT

In the sun-drenched island of Crete, we discovered a meat taverna called Apokoronas. The smoky char from the coal fire complemented the tender, juicy meat we were served there. The pickled pepper and shallot mixture is so special, it really is our favourite thing to eat with lamb chops. This recipe brings a taste of Crete to your table.

Feeds 4–6

salt flakes
16 lamb chops, about 1.2 kg (2 lb 10 oz) in total
1 loaf of sourdough bread, torn into chunks
olive oil, for drizzling

HERB MARINADE
125 ml (½ cup) olive oil
1 teaspoon dried Greek oregano
1 teaspoon dried mint
1 teaspoon sweet paprika

PICKLED PEPPER & SHALLOT
5 shallots, finely sliced
2 golden Greek pepperoncini, drained and finely chopped
2 tablespoons red wine vinegar
1 teaspoon salt flakes
1 teaspoon caster (superfine) sugar
1 tablespoon parsley leaves, finely chopped

In a large bowl, combine all the herb marinade ingredients and season with salt flakes. Add the lamb and turn to coat, then cover and marinate in the fridge overnight.

Combine all the pickled pepper and shallot ingredients in a bowl and set aside to pickle for 30 minutes.

Drizzle the bread chunks with olive oil and set aside.

Heat a chargrill pan or barbecue over high heat. Grill the lamb chops for 2–4 minutes on each side, until charred and cooked to your liking. Cover with foil and set aside to rest for about 5 minutes.

Wipe the grill clean. Toast the bread chunks on the grill for 30 seconds to 1 minute, until crispy and toasted.

Top the lamb chops with the pickled pepper and shallot and serve with the charred bread.

A NOTE ON PREP
The pickled pepper and shallot mixture can be prepared the day before and kept in the fridge in a covered glass bowl. Stir through the chopped parsley right before serving.

SERVE ME WITH
This makes a great afternoon spread with Melitzanosalata (page 25) and our Black-eyed bean salad (page 172) – washed down with our refreshing Pomegranate and mint spritz (page 238).

Honey Chicken Wings with Galotyri & Green Pepper Herby Oil

Our Aunt Christine has a real love of preparing chicken wings for her family; it's her signature dish. She combines the sweetness of Greek honey with the tanginess of galotyri cheese, which works so well together that we've used this magic combination in our chicken wings as well. Here we've paired them with a green pepper herby oil that has become a bit of a favourite for us.

In our cookbook *Peináo*, we served the green pepper herby oil with a potato salad. It's also perfect with lamb and chicken, so we just had to share the recipe with you.

Feeds 4-6

1 tablespoon olive oil
1 tablespoon honey
1 teaspoon dried dill
1 teaspoon smoked paprika
salt flakes
2 kg (4 lb 6 oz) chicken wings
180 g (6½ oz) galotyri cheese, or softened cream cheese

GREEN PEPPER HERBY OIL

80 ml (⅓ cup) extra virgin olive oil
100 g (3½ oz) golden Greek pepperoncini, drained
1 cup chopped parsley and dill fronds
1 tablespoon capers, drained
2 teaspoons white wine vinegar
1 teaspoon salt flakes

In a large bowl, combine the olive oil, honey, dill and paprika. Season with salt flakes and whisk to combine. Add the chicken wings and toss to coat. Cover and marinate in the fridge for at least 1 hour, or overnight.

Place all the green pepper herby oil ingredients in a food processor and whiz until roughly chopped. Set aside.

Heat a barbecue or chargrill pan over medium heat. Grill the chicken wings for 20 minutes, or until charred and cooked through, turning them every 5 minutes.

To serve, spread the galotyri onto a serving platter. Top with the chicken wings and drizzle with the green pepper herby oil.

A NOTE ON PREP
The chicken wings can be marinated in the fridge the day before, just bring them out an hour before cooking. The green pepper herby oil can be made several hours ahead and kept covered at room temperature.

SERVE ME WITH
A couple of cold Greek beers! The picked meat from the chicken wings is also delicious served on pita breads (page 26), spread the pita with galotyri and drizzle over the green pepper herby oil.

GRILLED LAMB'S LIVER WITH ONIONS

As kids, fried liver wasn't our favourite, but it's our mum's top pick and a hit with the older generation. When done properly, fried liver has a mild texture and subtle taste. It cooks fast, with just a few minutes on each side, and should retain a slightly pink centre. If overcooked, it can get tough. Soaking it in milk helps remove bitterness and tenderises it, too.

For this recipe you could also use chicken livers.

Place the liver and milk in a bowl and leave to soak for 45 minutes. Drain the liver and pat dry with paper towel.

Heat the olive oil in a large frying pan over medium heat. Add the onion, season with salt flakes and cook for 2–4 minutes, until softened and golden brown. Remove from the pan, set aside and keep warm.

Increase the heat to high and add the butter and liver to the pan. Cook the liver for 2–3 minutes on each side.

Remove the pan from the heat and allow the liver to rest for about 5 minutes.

Serve the liver on a serving plate with the pan-fried onion, lemon wedges and confit garlic cloves.

Feeds 4

500 g (1 lb 2 oz) lamb's liver, cut into 3 cm (1¼ in) chunks
250 ml (1 cup) full-cream (whole) milk
1 tablespoon olive oil
2 white onions, sliced into rounds
salt flakes
1 tablespoon unsalted butter
lemon wedges, to serve
Confit garlic cloves (page 26), to serve

A NOTE ON PREP
Liver is best cooked fresh, but it can be sliced and soaked in the milk several hours before serving.

SERVE ME WITH
Patates tiganites (page 34) and a Dakos salad (page 178).

TAVERNA DIARIES

TAVERNA KRONOS

THESSALONIKI

- LOCATION -
Thessaloniki

- ADDRESS -
178 Vassilissis Olgas and
Georgiou Vafopoulou 30,
Thessaloniki 546 46, Greece

- PHONE -
+30 231 041 4730

- RECIPE -
Soutzoukakia on the grill

Far from the bustling centre of the city, on Vasilissis Olgas Avenue in the charming neighbourhood of Ntepo, you will find <u>TAVERNA KRONOS</u>, an iconic taverna that is known for serving the best soutzoukakia (meatballs) in Thessaloniki. Prepared using the same recipe for over half a century, their amazing soutzoukakia has stood the test of time and gained worldwide recognition.

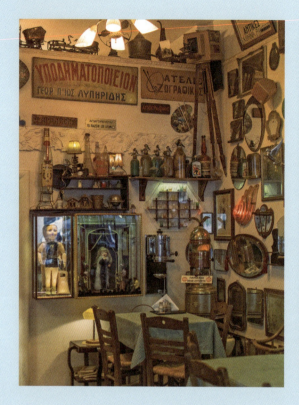

It all started back in 1960 when Sokratis Xristodoulou's father fell ill, and his illness made it hard to sustain the family's taverna due to his immense medical expenses, so they made the decision to shut it down. In a moment of hope, the struggling family bought a lottery ticket - which, amazingly, they won. Feeling their luck was changing, they decided to reopen the taverna, albeit on a smaller scale. As the years went by the taverna made a name for itself, so they slowly expanded, buying the piece of land next to them, then the neighbouring store as well. Kronos was growing into the charming taverna that welcomes diners today.

The taverna takes its name from the baths (loutra) that used to exist there. Back in the 1950s, the water supply in Greece was limited, so people had to go to a public bath house to have a shower, paying one drachma for hot water and a clean towel. The loutra that existed before the taverna was built was called Kronos, so many of the cafes, restaurants and cinemas in the area have all taken this name, including this iconic taverna.

You can find all of Thessaloniki's culture and tradition on the walls of this place, which are filled with signs from other cafes, lights and vintage bottle openers and pictures, which makes you feel as if you are travelling in time, but with Sokratis also collecting different pieces from across the world, the vibe has started to become a bit more international.

> "The people who are drawn here come for the quality, not to show off or be served the best glass of wine; they come here because it feels like home"

In Greek, the name of the taverna's most famous dish, soutzoukakia, means 'meat with a lot of spices', but it is actually a Turkish word. The owner's father came from a peninsula in Turkey, and brought the 'Mikrasiatiki' cuisine (from 'Mikra Asia', or 'Minor Asia') with him to Greece. It is a constant battle between Greeks and Turks as to which country was the first to invent this type of dish, but what we do know is that various combinations of meat are used, and the secret to the perfect soutzoukakia lies in the balance between the spices and meat - something known only by the chef.

Besides its signature dish, Kronos offers many traditional recipes, including revithia (Greek chickpea soup) and Gigantes plaki (page 134), with the sourcing of these ingredients showing their commitment to quality. The giant beans are from Prespes Lakes in northern Greece, and the chickpeas (garbanzo beans) are from a specific region in Larissa - which locals say are the only two places you should buy these legumes from.

The taverna craves one thing: simplicity. The staff are like a family and many have been working here for at least a decade. The people who are drawn here come for the quality, not to show off or be served the best glass of wine; they come here because it feels like home.

While the taverna's famous soutzoukakia recipe remains a closely guarded secret, after a good little chat over a few glasses of ouzo we managed to extract all the ingredients from them - and after testing this dish several times at home, we reckon this version gives you a real taste of those magical meatballs from Thessaloniki.

SOUTZOUKAKIA ON THE GRILL

Feeds 4; makes 12-14

MEATBALLS
550 g (1 lb 3 oz) fatty minced (ground) pork
250 g (9 oz) fatty minced (ground) beef
1 white onion, grated
½ cup finely chopped parsley leaves
50 g (½ cup) coarse dried breadcrumbs
2 teaspoons ground cumin
1 teaspoon ground coriander
1 teaspoon ground white pepper
1 teaspoon salt flakes, plus extra to serve
½ teaspoon ground sumac
¼ teaspoon freshly grated nutmeg
¼ teaspoon ground aniseed

TO SERVE
sliced white onion
chilli flakes
hot mustard
dried Greek oregano
roughly chopped parsley leaves
salt flakes

Place all the meatball ingredients in a large bowl. Using your hands, mix together well.

Roll 75 g (about 3 tablespoons/2¾ oz) portions of the mixture into oblong-shaped meatballs.

Heat a barbecue or chargrill pan over high heat. Cook the meatballs for 12 minutes, turning halfway through, or until charred and cooked all the way through. Remove from the heat, cover with foil and allow to rest for 10 minutes.

Serve with sliced white onion, chilli flakes, hot mustard, dried oregano, some roughly chopped parsley leaves and an extra sprinkle of salt flakes.

A NOTE ON PREP
The meatballs can be rolled and shaped a day ahead and kept covered in the fridge; this will also help the flavours develop.

SERVE ME WITH
We love turning these into a gyros with our pita breads from page 26, a dollop of Greek-style yoghurt, parsley leaves and sliced tomato. They are also great with Maroulosalata (page 171) and some fresh bread.

TAVERNA KRONOS

FROM THE

OVEN

ΜΑΓΕΙΡΕΥΤΑ

Moussaka, yemista (stuffed vegetables), oven-roasted lamb with potatoes, rooster in wine sauce … these are some of the classic Greek dishes we all know and love, collectively known as mageirefta. Either baked in the oven or simmered slowly on the stove, you'll often spot these traditional, soul-warming meals in bain-marie food warmers behind a glass display at your favourite local taverna. They're usually made fresh each day in limited quantities, so it's no surprise they often sell out quickly!

Think of the delicious lamb-stuffed eggplant dish Papoutsakia (page 149), the creamy-layered beef and pasta Pastitsio (page 145), and melt-in-your-mouth tender Lamb kleftiko (page 150) as being like a warm hug on a plate – they really are the go-to recipes for anyone wanting to bring that welcoming taverna vibe to their own home. The best part? Once you've done the prep for these recipes, you can let them cook away while you get the table ready for a cosy meal with your friends and family.

FROM THE OVEN

RICE-STUFFED ZUCCHINI FLOWERS
133

GIGANTES PLAKI
Greek giant baked beans
134

TAVERNA DIARIES:
TO STEKI TOU MACHERA, AMORGOS -
REVITHADA
Baked chickpeas
136

PEPPERS STUFFED WITH GREEK
CHEESES & SUN-DRIED TOMATO
142

BEEF PASTITSIO WITH
GRAVIERA BECHAMEL
145

PRESERVED LEMON ROASTED CHICKEN
WITH JAMMY LEEKS
146

PAPOUTSAKIA
Eggplant topped with lamb mince
and bechamel
149

LAMB KLEFTIKO WITH ROASTED
TOMATOES & POTATOES
150

HILOPITES WITH CHICKEN
152

SOUTZOUKAKIA
Pork and beef meatballs in
tomato sauce
155

BEEF STIFADO WITH BABY
WHOLE ONIONS
156

TAVERNA DIARIES:
NTOUNIAS, CRETE -
KATSIKAKI TSIGARIASTO
Goat in olive oil
158

RICE-STUFFED ZUCCHINI FLOWERS

These stuffed zucchini flowers are a true celebration of Greek summer, filled with a fragrant mixture of rice, fresh herbs and lemon. We still dream of the delicious ones we ate at Tamam restaurant in Chania, Crete. These beauties are delicate yet bursting with flavours of the Mediterranean.

This recipe uses female zucchini flowers, which have a small zucchini still attached to the flower. You can find them at green grocers or markets.

Preheat the oven to 170°C (340°F).

Warm half the olive oil in a large saucepan over medium heat. Fry the onion for 8–9 minutes, until softened. Add the garlic and oregano and cook for a further 5 minutes, or until softened. Add the grated tomatoes and zucchini stems and cook for 8 minutes, or until no excess water remains.

Add the rice and cook for 3 minutes. Stir in the herbs, cinnamon, cumin and lemon zest. Season with salt flakes and cracked pepper.

Pour the tomato passata into a round 25 cm (10 in) oven-safe baking dish or frying pan.

Using a spoon, carefully fill each zucchini flower with about 1 tablespoon of the rice mixture, gently twisting the tops of the flowers to enclose the filling. Carefully arrange the filled zucchini flowers on top of the tomato passata.

In a small jug, mix together the stock, lemon juice and remaining 2 tablespoons olive oil. Pour the mixture over the zucchini flowers.

Cover the dish with baking paper and foil, then place in the oven and bake for 1 hour.

Remove the foil and baking paper. Bake, uncovered, for a further 10 minutes, or until the zucchini flowers are lightly golden on top and the rice is cooked.

Feeds 4

- 80 ml (⅓ cup) olive oil
- 1 onion, finely chopped
- 2 garlic cloves, crushed
- 1 teaspoon dried Greek oregano
- 2 tomatoes, about 280 g (10 oz) in total, grated, skin discarded
- 20 female zucchini (courgette) flowers, small zucchini removed and finely grated
- 200 g (1 cup) long-grain white rice, washed well
- small handful of mixed mint and parsley leaves, chopped
- ¼ teaspoon ground cinnamon
- ¼ teaspoon ground cumin
- zest of 1 lemon, plus 1 teaspoon lemon juice
- salt flakes and freshly cracked black pepper
- 500 g (1 lb 2 oz) tomato passata (pureed tomatoes)
- 125 ml (½ cup) vegetable stock

A NOTE ON PREP
These zucchini flowers are best made fresh to serve.

SERVE ME WITH
For a vegetarian feast, serve alongside a Hortopita (page 183) and Revithokeftedes (page 42).

GIGANTES PLAKI
Greek giant baked beans

This is the 'I can eat this for breakfast, lunch and dinner' meal we could literally eat every day of the week. Cooked in the oven with all the spices and tomatoes, these beans hold so much flavour and are perfect with some feta crumbled on top.

Feeds 4–6

- 500 g (1 lb 2 oz) dried lima beans (butter beans)
- salt flakes
- 60 ml (¼ cup) olive oil, plus extra to serve
- 1 brown onion, sliced
- 3 garlic cloves, finely chopped
- 1 large red pepper (capsicum), chopped
- 2 large tomatoes, chopped
- 1 teaspoon dried Greek oregano
- 1 teaspoon smoked paprika
- 350 g (12½ oz) tomato passata (pureed tomatoes)
- 100 g (3½ oz) chopped silverbeet (Swiss chard) leaves

Place the beans in a large bowl and cover with 5 cm (2 in) cold water. Leave to soak overnight, or for at least 12 hours.

The following day, rinse the beans well with water at least three times, until the water runs clear. Place in a large saucepan with 3 litres (12 cups) water. Season with salt flakes and bring to the boil. Reduce the heat and simmer for 1½–2 hours, skimming the froth off the top as needed, until the beans are al dente but not mushy. Drain and set aside until needed.

Preheat the oven to 180°C (350°F).

Heat the olive oil in a saucepan over medium–low heat. Fry the onion for 8 minutes, or until slightly softened. Add the garlic, red pepper, tomatoes, oregano and paprika. Cook, stirring, for a further 10 minutes, or until softened. Stir the passata through, along with the cooked beans and silverbeet.

Transfer the mixture to a large baking dish. Cover with baking paper and foil, then bake for 45 minutes.

Remove the paper and foil and bake, uncovered, for a further 15 minutes, or until the beans are tender. Serve drizzled with olive oil.

A NOTE ON PREP
This is the perfect dish to have already made in the fridge. The following day, simply reheat on the stovetop over low heat until the beans are warmed through, adding some water if the beans are not saucy enough.

SERVE ME WITH
Lamb chops with pickled pepper and shallot (page 117) and Horiatiko psomi (page 59).

TAVERNA DIARIES

TO STEKI TOU MACHERA

AMORGOS

- LOCATION -
Amorgos

- ADDRESS -
Asfontilitis, 840 08 Amorgos, Greece

- PHONE -
+30 693 667 1031

- RECIPE -
Revithada (Baked chickpeas)

Long and narrow with towering cliffs, Amorgos is the seventh largest island in the Cyclades, and is known as the 'hidden island' by locals - and when you arrive you can understand why. One of the more remote and less touristy Greek islands, Amorgos lies east of Naxos and is known for its dramatic landscapes, clear waters and traditional villages. One of the island's highlights is the iconic 11th century Monastery of Hozoviotissa, a whitewashed building clinging to a cliffside overlooking the Aegean Sea which is dedicated to the Virgin Mary. Another highlight is a hidden gem of a taverna called TO STEKI TOU MACHERA, which we had been told we needed to visit when we arrived on Amorgos.

To Steki tou Machera is somewhat off the beaten path, up a winding unmarked road, and the property has no wifi, which adds to the taverna's charm once you manage to find it.

For the past 12 years, this taverna has been welcoming guests from May to October, run by a remarkable woman in her seventies named Kyria Sofia, who cooks the most delicious chickpeas (garbanzo beans) in her wood-fired oven.

Travellers from all over the world come to visit this serene spot on Amorgos, perched up in the mountains just a little way from the port. Visitors are drawn by the captivating views and Kyria Sofia's homely meals that are made with the island's finest ingredients including fava (split peas), goat, lamb and capers.

Kyria Sofia cooks every dish with love and 'meraki' - the Greek word for doing something with soul, creativity and passion, and says the whole taverna reminds her of her father. It was her father who suggested, over 20 years ago, turning this piece of land in the mountains into a psilikatzidiko (small convenience store), being located along a main road where most tourists passed. At first Kyria Sofia dismissed the idea, but a year after her father died, she felt the need to pay tribute to him by opening this taverna, which she named after his nickname, 'Maxairas'.

Everything is cooked by Kyria Sofia herself in a traditional outdoor wood-fired oven. By 7 am, she's already at work, and by 8 am, her unique dishes are slowly cooking to perfection. But you can't just rock up and expect her to have enough food for you - as Kyria Sofia only cooks the right amount of food to cater for those who have called beforehand to make a booking. On the menu are a variety of different dishes, such as kotopoulo lemonato (lemon chicken), pastitsio (Greek pasta bake), yemista (stuffed vegetables with rice), katsikaki giouvetsi (baked goat with orzo) - and her personal favourite, revithada (baked chickpeas), which diners also love and are a traditional part of the island's diet.

"Kyria Sofia cooks every dish with love and 'meraki' – the Greek word for doing something with soul, creativity and passion"

Kyria Sofia's approach to cooking is simple and practical; her method ensures zero waste and best taste! Her dishes are served fresh from the oven, as soon as the guests arrive. When she has a larger reservation of 15 people, she often prepares her specialty – goat stuffed with liver and rice, a truly unforgettable dish. Despite the long hours, from early morning until 10 pm, Kyria Sofia is never tired, her dishes and loyal customers reflecting her passion and dedication to her cooking craft.

Her ingredients are as authentic and warm as she is, usually sourced from her own farm where she raises livestock and grows vegetables. Kyria Sofia loves bringing her charisma and hospitality to every table, sitting down with her guests, getting to know them, sharing stories about herself and her taverna and how it came to life.

Months before visiting Kyria Sofia, we had called to ask if she would be willing to share with us one of her recipes for this book. She was so welcoming when we arrived, it brought tears to our eyes seeing her explain the following recipe with so much love.

REVITHADA
Baked chickpeas

Serves 4–6

500 g (1 lb 2 oz) dried chickpeas (garbanzo beans)
1 tablespoon baking soda
1 tablespoon salt
1 long bullhorn (banana) pepper, chopped
2 large tomatoes, chopped
1 brown onion, chopped
125 ml (½ cup) olive oil
½ teaspoon ground turmeric
½ teaspoon sweet paprika
375 ml (1½ cups) water

Place the chickpeas in a large saucepan with the baking soda and salt. Cover with water and allow the chickpeas to soak, uncovered, at room temperature overnight.

The following day, drain the chickpeas and rinse under cold running water until the water runs clear. Place the chickpeas in a large saucepan over medium heat, pour in fresh water to cover and bring to the boil. Reduce the heat and simmer, uncovered, for 20 minutes, or until the chickpeas are tender but still holding their shape, now and then skimming off any white foam that rises to the surface.

Meanwhile, preheat the oven to 160°C (320°F).

Drain the chickpeas and place in a large baking dish. Add the remaining ingredients and mix to combine. Cover with foil and bake for 2 hours, or until the chickpeas are tender. Remove the foil and bake uncovered for a further 30 minutes, or until the chickpeas are lightly golden.

Serve with fresh bread to mop up all those beautiful juices.

NOTE
Kyria Sofia bakes her chickpeas in a wood-fired oven, which is much hotter than a regular oven and cooks more quickly. The recipe she has provided here is an easier version for a standard home oven.

A NOTE ON PREP
You'll need to start this recipe the day before to soak the dried chickpeas overnight.

SERVE ME WITH
For a vegetarian feast, serve the chickpeas with slices of the Horiatiko psomi (page 59) alongside our Peppers stuffed with Greek cheeses and sun-dried tomato (page 142), Hortopita (page 183) and a refreshing glass of The Med (page 235).

TO STEKI TOU MACHERA

Peppers Stuffed with Greek Cheeses & Sun-Dried Tomato

The smell of roasted peppers truly brings back memories of Yiayia's kitchen. She would pickle them, stuff them or enjoy them sliced fresh in a salad. Her cheese filling was always simple, but we've added goat's cheese and sun-dried tomatoes here for even more flavour.

Preheat the oven to 200°C (400°F). Line a large baking tray with baking paper.

In a bowl, mix together the goat's cheese, feta, sun-dried tomato and oregano leaves. Season with salt flakes and cracked pepper.

Cut off and reserve the tops of the peppers. Discard the internal seeds and white membranes.

Using the handle end of a spoon, fill the peppers with the cheese mixture, making sure to get as much filling inside as possible. Put the lids on and skewer with toothpicks to secure them in place. Arrange on the baking tray and drizzle with the olive oil.

Roast for 30–35 minutes, until the peppers have softened and are lightly golden.

Feeds 4-6

- 150 g (5½ oz) goat's cheese, crumbled
- 150 g (5½ oz) Greek feta, crumbled
- 35 g (¼ cup) sun-dried tomatoes in olive oil, drained and finely chopped
- small handful of chopped fresh oregano leaves
- salt flakes and freshly cracked black pepper
- 10 whole bullhorn (banana) peppers, about 700 g (1 lb 9 oz) in total
- 60 ml (¼ cup) olive oil

A NOTE ON PREP
The peppers can be filled with the cheese mixture and kept in the fridge overnight. When ready to serve, bring to room temperature and bake as directed.

SERVE ME WITH
Sardines with tomato and marjoram (page 71) and warm marinated olives.

FROM THE OVEN

BEEF PASTITSIO WITH GRAVIERA BECHAMEL

Can pastitsio be our favourite recipe? Maybe, because of our memories attached to those smells wafting from the kitchen. When Papou would collect us from school, the first question we'd ask was what Yiayia had made for dinner. 'I'm not sure,' he would answer, 'I have been busy mowing the lawns.' Even our school friend knew about Yiayia's pastitsio – she was known for it.

Feeds 6-8

500 g (1 lb 2 oz) bucatini, such as Misko Pastitsio No. 2
olive oil, for drizzling
100 g (3½ oz) kefalotyri cheese, grated
60 g (2 oz) graviera cheese, grated

BOLOGNESE SAUCE
60 ml (¼ cup) olive oil
1 brown onion, chopped
2 garlic cloves, sliced
small handful of fresh oregano leaves, chopped
600 g (1 lb 5 oz) minced (ground) beef
1 teaspoon ground cinnamon
1 teaspoon dried dill
salt flakes and freshly cracked black pepper
1 tablespoon tomato paste (concentrated puree)
125 ml (½ cup) red wine, or beef stock
2 fresh bay leaves
400 g (14 oz) tinned crushed tomatoes

GRAVIERA BECHAMEL
120 g (4½ oz) unsalted butter
90 g (3 oz) plain (all-purpose) flour
1.1 litres (37 fl oz) full-cream (whole) milk, warmed
3 egg yolks
60 g (2 oz) graviera cheese, grated
¼ teaspoon ground or freshly grated nutmeg

Preheat the oven to 180°C (350°F).

To make the bolognese sauce, heat the olive oil in a large saucepan over low heat and cook the onion for 8 minutes, or until softened. Add the garlic and oregano and cook for a further 2 minutes. Add the beef, cinnamon and dill. Season with salt flakes and cook, stirring, for another 8 minutes, or until the beef is browned. Stir in the tomato paste and cook for a further 2 minutes. Pour in the wine (or beef stock), add the bay leaves and simmer for 5 minutes, or until the wine has reduced by half. Stir in the crushed tomatoes, along with 250 ml (1 cup) water, then simmer for 30 minutes, or until the sauce has thickened.

Cook the pasta in a large saucepan of boiling salted water, following the packet instructions. Drain, then drizzle with olive oil to stop the pasta sticking together.

To make the bechamel, melt the butter in a saucepan over low heat. Add the flour and cook, stirring, for 3 minutes, or until the flour has cooked out and the mixture has formed a paste. Whisking constantly, gradually pour in the milk a little at a time, until the sauce starts to thicken. Bring to a simmer and whisk in the egg yolks, graviera cheese and nutmeg. Season with salt flakes and cracked pepper and cook, stirring constantly, for 15–20 minutes, until the bechamel becomes thick and glossy.

To assemble the pastitsio, you'll need a 23 cm × 34 cm (9 in × 13½ in) baking dish that is at least 7 cm (2¾ in) deep. Start by layering half the pasta on the base. Scatter with one-third of the kefalotyri cheese, one-third of the bechamel and a layer of the beef mixture. Repeat to make another layer. Top with the remaining bechamel and kefalotyri, then scatter with the graviera.

Bake, uncovered, for 35–40 minutes, until the top is golden brown.

A NOTE ON PREP
The entire dish can be assembled the day before, ready for baking. The next day, bring the dish to room temperature, then bake as directed.

SERVE ME WITH
No pastitsio is complete without a side of Horiatiki salata (page 168).

PRESERVED LEMON ROASTED CHICKEN WITH JAMMY LEEKS

The humble roast chicken is a staple in our homes. Smearing butter underneath the skin will create a juicy chicken, and will also give you deliciously crispy skin. Preserved lemon has a unique citrus flavour that works beautifully with chicken, and is readily available from delicatessens and good produce stores. Leeks that have been cooked slowly in butter and chicken pan juices really are the yummiest leeks you will ever taste.

Feeds 4

- 100 g (3½ oz) unsalted butter, softened
- 2 Confit garlic cloves (page 26), mashed, or 2 crushed garlic cloves
- 2 preserved lemon quarters, rind finely chopped
- 6 lemon thyme sprigs, leaves picked
- salt flakes and freshly cracked black pepper
- 3 leeks, tops trimmed, washed well and halved down the middle
- 1 × 2 kg (4 lb 6 oz) whole chicken
- 1 tablespoon olive oil
- 250 ml (1 cup) chicken stock

In a bowl, mix together the butter, confit garlic cloves, preserved lemon and lemon thyme leaves. Season with salt flakes and cracked pepper.

Preheat the oven to 220°C (430°F). Arrange the leeks in a large baking dish.

Using your fingers, carefully loosen the skin from the flesh of the chicken breasts and thighs. Spread the butter mixture as evenly as possible under the skin.

Place the chicken on top of the leeks. Tie the chicken legs together with kitchen twine. Drizzle the chicken with the olive oil, then pour the chicken stock over the leeks.

Roast for about 1¼ hours, turning the dish around once to evenly brown the chicken. To check the chicken is cooked, insert a skewer into the thickest part of the thigh; the juices should run clear.

Remove the chicken from the oven, cover with foil and allow to rest for about 10 minutes.

Carve the chicken and serve with the jammy leeks and pan juices.

A NOTE ON PREP
The chicken is best roasted on the day of serving, but the butter mixture can be made ahead and spread under the chicken skin the night before roasting. Refrigerate the chicken overnight, but make sure to bring it out at least 30 minutes before cooking to bring it to room temperature.

SERVE ME WITH
Patatosalata (page 174) and Maroulosalata (page 171).

PAPOUTSAKIA
Eggplant topped with lamb mince and bechamel

Papoutsakia translates to 'little shoes', and is quite similar in flavour to a moussaka, minus the potato component. Growing up, Mum and Yiayia would cook a lot of lamb dishes – and this particular recipe was requested often. For a vegetarian option, swap the lamb for tinned brown lentils.

Feeds 4-6

4 eggplants (aubergines), halved lengthways
salt flakes and freshly cracked black pepper
80 ml (⅓ cup) extra virgin olive oil
1 white onion, finely chopped
3 garlic cloves, crushed
500 g (1 lb 2 oz) minced (ground) lamb
1 tablespoon dried Greek oregano
½ teaspoon ground cinnamon
½ teaspoon ground cumin
400 g (14 oz) tinned diced tomatoes
60 g (¼ cup) tomato paste (concentrated puree)
80 g (1 cup) fresh breadcrumbs
grated kefalotyri cheese, for sprinkling
small handful of fresh oregano leaves

BECHAMEL
80 g (2¾ oz) unsalted butter
50 g (⅓ cup) plain (all-purpose) flour, sifted
750 ml (3 cups) full-cream (whole) milk, warmed
2 large egg yolks
40 g (1½ oz) kefalotyri cheese, grated, plus extra to serve

Preheat the oven to 200°C (400°F). Line a baking tray with baking paper.

Using a sharp knife, cut deep incisions into the flesh side of the eggplant halves, about 1 cm (½ in) apart, in a cross-hatch pattern. Season the flesh with salt flakes and drizzle with 2 tablespoons of the olive oil.

Place on the baking tray, skin side up, and bake for 20–30 minutes, until the eggplant halves have softened but are still holding their shape. Remove from the oven and set aside.

Meanwhile, heat the remaining oil in a deep saucepan over medium heat. Add the onion and cook for 8 minutes, or until softened. Add the garlic, lamb, oregano, cinnamon and cumin and cook, stirring, for 8–10 minutes. Stir in the tomatoes, tomato paste and 125 ml (½ cup) water. Cook for 30 minutes, or until the sauce has thickened, stirring now and then. Season with salt flakes and cracked pepper and set aside.

For the bechamel, melt the butter in a small saucepan over medium heat. Add the flour and cook, stirring constantly, for 2–4 minutes, until a paste forms. Gradually add the milk, whisking constantly, and cook for 10–12 minutes, until it starts to thicken. Whisk in the egg yolks and cheese. Season with salt flakes and cracked pepper and cook, whisking, for a further 10–15 minutes, until thick and creamy.

Meanwhile, heat the oven grill (broiler) to 220°C (430°F).

Divide the lamb mixture among the eggplant halves. Top with the bechamel and scatter with the breadcrumbs and some grated kefalotyri cheese. Grill for 10 minutes, or until the bechamel is lightly golden and the cheese has melted.

Scatter with the oregano leaves to serve.

A NOTE ON PREP
The lamb filling and bechamel can both be made the day before and kept in the fridge. Just cover the top of the bechamel with plastic wrap, to stop a skin forming. There's no need to reheat the bechamel; simply bring it back to room temperature, then scoop straight onto the lamb mixture just before grilling.

SERVE ME WITH
Our Maroulosalata (page 171) is crisp and fresh and exactly what a rich dish like this needs. Don't forget a glass of white or red wine; xinomavro is a favourite red variety of ours.

LAMB KLEFTIKO WITH ROASTED TOMATOES & POTATOES

Lamb kleftiko translates to 'thief's lamb'. The name originates from the Klephts, who stole lambs and cooked them in underground ovens, so all the smells wouldn't escape and their stolen bounty would remain a secret. Wrapped in baking paper to seal all the delicious juices, it's our favourite way to cook and eat lamb leg.

Feeds 4-6

- salt flakes and freshly cracked black pepper
- 2.2 kg (5 lb) leg of lamb, bone in
- 800 g (1 lb 12 oz) chat (baby) potatoes, larger potatoes halved
- 2 garlic bulbs, halved horizontally
- 1 red onion, cut into thin wedges
- 300 g (10½ oz) cherry tomatoes
- 1 teaspoon dried Greek oregano
- 1 tablespoon olive oil

LEMON & OREGANO MARINADE
- 3 garlic cloves
- 1 teaspoon salt flakes
- 60 ml (¼ cup) lemon juice
- 1 teaspoon ground cinnamon
- 1 teaspoon dried Greek oregano
- ¼ bunch of oregano, leaves picked and chopped
- freshly cracked black pepper
- 60 ml (¼ cup) olive oil

To make the marinade, use a mortar and pestle to crush together the garlic cloves and salt flakes. Add the lemon juice, cinnamon, dried oregano and fresh oregano. Season with cracked pepper and grind a little more until finely crushed, then stir the olive oil through.

Place the lamb in a large roasting tin. Pour the marinade over, then cover and leave to marinate for 2 hours, or even overnight in the fridge.

Preheat the oven to 160°C (320°F). Lay two long pieces of baking paper on top of each other – one widthways, the other lengthways, to form a cross. Carefully place in a large roasting tin.

Add the potatoes, garlic bulb halves, onion wedges and cherry tomatoes to the roasting tin. Season with the dried oregano, salt flakes and cracked pepper, then drizzle with the olive oil and 60 ml (¼ cup) water.

Place the marinated lamb leg on top of the vegetables. Fold the baking paper over, then cover with foil to completely enclose the lamb. Roast for 3 hours, then increase the oven temperature to 200°C (400°F) and roast for a further 1 hour, or until the meat is tender.

Remove the foil and baking paper and roast for a further 20 minutes, until the lamb is golden brown and crispy.

Allow the lamb to rest for about 15 minutes, then slice and serve with the potatoes, garlic and tomatoes.

A NOTE ON PREP
Marinating the lamb the night before will enhance the flavour and help tenderise the meat, just make sure you bring the lamb back to room temperature before placing it in the oven.

SERVE ME WITH
A big bowl of garlicky Tzatziki (page 114) to dip the lamb pieces into. If you're lucky to have any leftovers, make a lamb gyros by smashing the potatoes into warm pita breads and topping with sliced tomato, onion and parsley.

HILOPITES WITH CHICKEN

Usually used in soups or paired with meat, 'hilopites' are a small, square, flat Greek pasta, traditionally made in villages using flour, eggs and milk. During summer when it's warm outside, Mum's cousin Eleni makes her own hilopites, ready to enjoy when the cold weather arrives. Eleni begins by making a dough, rolling it into a thin sheet before cutting the dough into small squares with a knife. The scene is absolutely beautiful – tables are covered with tablecloths and scattered with hilopites, while the Greek sun shines overhead and helps dry the pasta.

Many traditional tavernas serve hilopites with rooster cooked in a tomato and wine sauce (kokora krasato). Our take on this dish uses chicken drumsticks, which work beautifully and are much more readily available.

You can find hilopites in most Greek delicatessens.

Preheat the oven to 180°C (350°F).

Heat half the olive oil in a large ovenproof frying pan or cast-iron saucepan over medium heat. Season the chicken with salt flakes and sear on both sides for 5 minutes, until the skin is golden brown. Remove the chicken from the pan and set aside.

Add the remaining olive oil to the pan and cook the onion for 8 minutes, or until softened. Add the garlic, spices and bay leaves and cook for 2 minutes. Stir in the tomato paste and cook for a further 2 minutes, or until fragrant.

Return the chicken to the pan. Pour in the tomato passata and 125 ml (½ cup) boiling water and bring to a simmer. Cover with the lid, transfer the pan to the oven and bake for 1 hour.

Remove the pan from the oven and remove the lid. Scatter the hilopites into the saucy parts, making sure to coat all the pasta in the sauce. Pour 1 cup (250 ml) boiling water over.

Place back into the oven, uncovered, and bake for a further 15 minutes, or until the pasta is soft to the bite.

Remove from the oven, put the lid back on and allow to sit for 10 minutes before serving.

Feeds 4-6

- 60 ml (¼ cup) extra virgin olive oil
- 8 chicken drumsticks, skin on
- salt flakes
- 1 brown onion, finely chopped
- 2 garlic cloves, chopped
- ½ teaspoon sweet paprika
- ½ teaspoon ground cumin
- ½ teaspoon ground cinnamon
- 2 fresh or dried bay leaves
- 1 tablespoon tomato paste (concentrated puree)
- 700 g (1 lb 9 oz) tomato passata (pureed tomatoes)
- 330 g (1½ cups) dried hilopites

A NOTE ON PREP
This recipe is best made fresh on the day it's to be served. If heating leftovers, add a little water to the pan and gently warm over low heat.

SERVE ME WITH
Stuffed fried olives (page 45), Beetroot with mizithra cheese (page 177) and a Pomegranate and mint spritz (page 238).

FROM THE OVEN

SOUTZOUKAKIA
Pork and beef meatballs in tomato sauce

This classic dish is enjoyed in many Greek and Turkish homes and is perfect on a wintry day – it's a comforting recipe when we are feeling a bit homesick. The cumin and cinnamon add warmth to the soutzoukakia, along with fresh herbs, and it is often served with fluffy, buttery rice or roasted potatoes.

Be sure not to use lean minced meat here, as this will make the soutzoukakia dry. Our yiayia would always use a mix of pork and beef together, as they both have a good amount of fat.

Preheat the oven to 200°C (400°F). Lightly grease a large baking dish.

To make the tomato sauce, heat the olive oil in a saucepan over medium heat and cook the onion for 8 minutes, or until softened. Stir in the garlic, oregano, crushed tomatoes and water. Reduce the heat to low and simmer for 20 minutes, or until reduced and thickened.

Meanwhile, in a large bowl, combine the pork, beef, onion, garlic, fresh and dried oregano, cumin, cinnamon, breadcrumbs, egg and olive oil. Season with salt flakes and cracked pepper. Knead the mixture for 2–3 minutes, until well combined. Using 2 tablespoons of the mixture at a time, roll the mixture into oblong-shaped meatballs.

Arrange the meatballs in the baking dish in two single layers. Pour the tomato sauce evenly over the top. Bake for 35–40 minutes, until the meatballs are cooked through and golden brown.

Serve the meatballs and tomato sauce on a bed of rice (see note below), drizzled with a little extra olive oil and with feta slices on the side.

Feeds 4-6

- 500 g (1 lb 2 oz) minced (ground) pork
- 500 g (1 lb 2 oz) minced (ground) beef
- 1 white onion, grated
- 2 garlic cloves, crushed
- small handful of chopped fresh oregano leaves
- 1 teaspoon dried Greek oregano
- 1 teaspoon ground cumin
- ½ teaspoon ground cinnamon
- 80 g (1 cup) fresh breadcrumbs
- 1 egg, lightly beaten
- 1 tablespoon olive oil, plus extra to serve
- salt flakes and freshly cracked black pepper
- fluffy, buttery white rice, to serve
- 100 g (3½ oz) Greek feta, cut into 1 cm (½ in) thick slices

TOMATO SAUCE
- 1 tablespoon olive oil
- 1 brown onion, roughly chopped
- 1 garlic clove, crushed
- 1 tablespoon chopped fresh oregano leaves
- 800 g (1 lb 12 oz) tinned crushed tomatoes
- 60 ml (¼ cup) water

A NOTE ON PREP
The meatballs and tomato sauce can both be made the day before and kept covered in the fridge. Remove the meatball mixture from the fridge 30 minutes before cooking.

SERVE ME WITH
Fluffy, buttery white rice, like our yiayia would make it. Rinse 300 g (1½ cups) medium-grain white rice until the water runs clear. Melt 70 g (2½ oz) salted butter in a saucepan with a lid over low heat, then add the rice and toast for 5 minutes, stirring frequently. Pour in 750 ml (3 cups) chicken broth or vegetable stock and bring to the boil. Reduce the heat to low, cover with a lid and simmer for 15 minutes, being sure not to remove the lid during the cooking time. Turn the heat off and allow the rice to sit for 20 minutes, then fluff the grains up with a fork and serve.

BEEF STIFADO WITH BABY WHOLE ONIONS

The smell of a beef stew bubbling away during winter is very comforting. Mum really loves beef stifado, so we always make it for her when she visits Sydney; paired with a Greek red wine and a loaf of bread, it's her ideal Saturday night. Make sure to brown the baby onions in the oil nicely as this helps them take on a lot of flavour.

Preheat the oven to 180°C (350°F).

Heat the olive oil in a large cast-iron saucepan over medium heat and sear the beef in batches for 8 minutes, or until browned. Remove the beef and set aside. Add the onions and fry for 10 minutes, turning often, until lightly browned and golden all over.

Return the beef to the pan, along with the wine, cinnamon sticks, bay leaves, allspice, cloves and tomato paste. Cook for 5 minutes, then stir in the crushed tomatoes and 250 ml (1 cup) water. Gently simmer for 5 minutes.

Cover with a lid, then place the pan in the oven. Bake for 2 hours, or until the beef is tender and falling apart, and the onions are soft.

Feeds 4

- 2 tablespoons olive oil
- 1 kg (2 lb 3 oz) beef chuck steak, cut into 5 cm (2 in) chunks
- 10 baby onions, peeled
- 250 ml (1 cup) red wine
- 2 cinnamon sticks
- 2 fresh or dried bay leaves
- ½ teaspoon ground allspice
- ¼ teaspoon ground cloves
- 2 tablespoons tomato paste (concentrated puree)
- 400 g (14 oz) tinned crushed tomatoes

A NOTE ON PREP
The entire dish can be cooked the day before and reheated just before guests arrive.

SERVE ME WITH
Stifado needs a glass of xinomavro (a Greek red wine). A loaf of our Horiatiko psomi (page 59) would also make a fine addition to the table. For dessert, serve something warm, such as Spiced almond and pistachio kataifi (page 211).

FROM THE OVEN 157

NTOUNIAS is a farm-to-table taverna where Cretan food traditions are brought to life. The moment you arrive at this remarkable eatery in the tree-lined village of Drakona, about 100 kilometres (62 miles) from the port city of Chania, you know you're in for something special. Outside the simple stone building, there's a modest wood-fire cooking station with pots bubbling away over open flames. The air is filled with the mouthwatering aroma of slow-cooked meats and the unmistakable sound of potatoes frying in oil. In the background there's a glimpse of the family's four-acre farmstead, and you might even spot a brood of chickens wandering by.

This cosy farm-to-table spot is the heart and soul of Stelios Trilirakis, a chef who chose tradition over the fast pace of city kitchens. In 2004, Stelios decided to leave his career in the city of Chania and return to his village, where he transformed his family's small taverna into a place that would keep alive the recipes and food traditions his grandmother taught him. Here, it's not just about the food - it's about savouring the flavours, traditions, and warmth of Crete in every bite.

Stelios' approach to food is all about staying close to nature and embracing what each harvest has to offer. He chooses to focus on what's in season, letting each ingredient shine without too much fuss. Stelios is a man of few words and is as down-to-earth as they come. He believes that great food doesn't need fancy techniques - just respect for the ingredients and a lot of heart. His philosophy is simple: keep things sustainable, and rooted in the community. Speaking of which, we love that he collaborates closely with local producers of honey, olive oil and wine, helping to support and strengthen the local community.

Stelios grows most of the restaurant's produce himself, and every vegetable, egg and cut of meat is as fresh as it gets, making the dining experience truly farm-to-table. He's passionate about eating with the seasons and respecting the land, which is a way of life in Crete.

At Ntounias, there's not a single modern appliance in sight. Everything is cooked using wood fires, just like generations gone by. Watching dishes come to life over the flames is mesmerising, with each dish getting the time it needs. When the food arrives, you know it's been made with love, inviting you to slow down and really savour it.

"Every vegetable, egg and cut of meat is as fresh as it gets, making the dining experience truly farm-to-table"

When we joined the other diners in the spacious rustic outdoor wooden gazebo that is the taverna's main eating area, our meal kicked off with bread - of course! Baked with four different flours and full of rustic, earthy flavour, it was an inviting start to the meal. We then sampled the tourlou, a flavourful veggie medley that's a lighter take on traditional briam (baked vegetables). This version really lets the fresh flavours of the vegetables shine through.

At Ntounias, Stelios' tsigariasto (goat stew) is next level, made using organic free-roaming goat and slow-cooked over a wood fire in clay pots for hours, giving it a deep, smoky dimension. The resulting meat is both tender and rich, with layers of flavour that are earthy, hearty and unforgettable. This dish is a true reflection of Crete's rustic culinary heritage, where simple ingredients are transformed into extraordinary meals through time, patience and respect for tradition. Even though this recipe doesn't use a wood fire or clay pot like the taverna does, Stelios has shared a version that you can make in your own kitchen at home.

Ntounias is one of those rare gems where everything - from the wood-fired cooking to the home-grown ingredients - comes from a real love for the land and Cretan traditions. It's more than just a taverna or a restaurant; it's a place that lets you slow down and soak up Crete's culture and flavours in the most authentic way. Here, you're not just eating; you're connecting with the island's history and savouring food made with heart. It's an experience that leaves you feeling truly nourished and inspired.

KATSIKAKI TSIGARIASTO
Goat in olive oil

Serves 4-6

60 ml (¼ cup) extra virgin olive oil
2 kg (4 lb 6 oz) goat shoulder, bone in, cut into 8-10 cm (3¼-4 in) chunks by your butcher
salt flakes and freshly cracked black pepper
400 ml (13½ fl oz) white wine
750 ml (3 cups) water

Preheat the oven to 160°C (320°F).

Pour the olive oil into a large, deep flameproof casserole dish over medium heat. Working in batches, fry the goat chunks on both sides for 4-5 minutes, until browned. Season with salt flakes and cracked pepper.

Pour the wine into the dish and return all the goat chunks to the dish. Reduce the heat to low and add the water. Cover with a lid, transfer the dish to the oven and bake for 4 hours, or until the goat is tender and falling off the bone.

Serve the goat with spoonfuls of the beautiful juices drizzled over.

A NOTE ON PREP
This dish can be made the day before, left to cool completely, then kept covered in the fridge. Gently reheat in the oven for serving.

SERVE ME WITH
White fluffy rice to mop up all those lovely juices, and a side of Beetroot with mizithra cheese (page 177). Or make goat gyros using our pita breads (page 26), finely sliced white onion, cucumber ribbons and a dollop of htipiti - a spread made with feta, roasted red peppers (capsicums) and red chilli (for a milder flavour, simply omit the chilli).

VEGETABLES

ΛΑΧΑΝΙΚΑ

Vegetables are truly at the heart of Greek cooking. When you step into a Greek taverna, you'll find no shortage of fresh, seasonal vegetable dishes. While some might think of them as just side dishes to meat or seafood, they're also a godsend for anyone following a plant-based diet, there is always a wide array of flavour-packed options for vegetarians and vegans. Greek cuisine keeps things simple, allowing the natural tastes of tomatoes, eggplants (aubergines), zucchini (courgettes) and greens to shine through with basic techniques such as grilling, roasting and slow-cooking.

Think of classics such as Horiatiki salata (page 168) or tangy, crunchy Dakos salad (page 178) – these dishes are all about letting the vegetables do the talking. Legumes are also a big deal on taverna menus, with comforting dishes like Black-eyed bean salad (page 172) and Bamies (page 184) serving up hearty, satisfying bites. As an added plus, many of these dishes are even better the next day, making for an amazing lunch.

One of our all-time favourite combinations at a Greek taverna is the simple yet perfect pairing of boiled beetroot (beets) and horta (wild greens). We've given these our own twist with our roasted Beetroot with mizithra cheese dish (page 177), which would pair perfectly with a delicious Hortopita (page 183).

Greece's love for fresh vegetables not only brings out the best seasonal flavours in their food, but also embodies what Greek eating is all about – being healthy, sustainable, and best enjoyed with good company.

VEGETABLES

HORIATIKI SALATA
Village salad
168

MAROULOSALATA
Lettuce salad
171

BLACK-EYED BEAN SALAD
172

PATATOSALATA
Herby potato salad
174

BEETROOT WITH MIZITHRA CHEESE
177

DAKOS SALAD
178

PATATES LEMONATES
Lemon potatoes
180

HORTOPITA
Greens pie
183

BAMIES
Okra with tomatoes
184

TAVERNA DIARIES:
TAVERNA OIKONOMOU, ATHENS -
LAHANODOLMADES
Cabbage rolls with avgolemono
186

HORIATIKI SALATA
Village salad

Feeds 4

- salt flakes and freshly cracked black pepper
- 1 large short cucumber, cut into thick rounds
- 250 g (9 oz) tomatoes, cut into chunks
- 1 bullhorn (banana) pepper, finely sliced
- 1 white onion, finely sliced
- 60 g (2 oz) mixed olives
- 200 g (7 oz) Greek feta, cut into chunks
- 40 g (1½ oz) caperberries, drained
- 75 g (2¾ oz) golden Greek pepperoncini, drained (optional)
- 1 teaspoon dried Greek oregano
- fresh oregano leaves, for sprinkling

LEMON DRESSING
- 80 ml (⅓ cup) extra virgin olive oil
- juice of 1 lemon
- 1 teaspoon dried Greek oregano

It would almost be illegal to not serve a Greek salad with every recipe in this book – besides the desserts, of course. Get your hands on some ripe, sweet tomatoes, never keep them in the fridge, and remember to have a good loaf of bread handy to mop up all the luscious tomato and oil juices.

Place all lemon dressing ingredients in a jar. Pop the lid on and give the dressing a good shake. Season with salt flakes and cracked pepper.

Place the cucumber in a bowl with the tomato, banana pepper, onion and olives. Add the dressing and gently toss using your hands.

Transfer the salad to a large serving plate, then top with the remaining ingredients.

A NOTE ON PREP
The dressing can be made the night before and stored in the fridge.

SERVE ME WITH
We believe every main meal should be accompanied by a Greek salad!

MAROULOSALATA
Lettuce salad

We love the simplicity of this salad – fresh, crisp lettuce leaves paired with a simple dressing that sings with the quintessential Greek flavours of olive oil, oregano and lemon juice. Chopping the lettuce leaves thinly is important, as is massaging the dressing into the lettuce leaves. Yiayia would use a paring knife to slice her lettuce in her hands, using no chopping board, and on hot summer days she would eat the lettuce just as it is.

Place the lettuce, spring onions and herbs in a large salad bowl and mix to combine.

To make the dressing, combine the olive oil, dried oregano and lemon juice in a small bowl. Season with salt flakes and cracked pepper and whisk to combine.

Pour the dressing over the lettuce and give it a good massage. Crumble the feta into the salad and serve.

Feeds 4

- 1 large cos (romaine) lettuce, washed well, finely sliced
- 3 spring onions (scallions), finely sliced
- ¼ bunch of dill, leaves picked
- ¼ bunch of chervil, leaves picked
- 60 ml (¼ cup) extra virgin olive oil
- ½ teaspoon dried Greek oregano
- 2 tablespoons lemon juice
- salt flakes and freshly cracked black pepper
- 100 g (3½ oz) Greek feta

A NOTE ON PREP
The dressing can be made ahead and refrigerated in a clean glass jar for up to 1 week.

SERVE ME WITH
We love having this with our Snapper with avgolemono and charred horta (page 75).

BLACK-EYED BEAN SALAD

Beans and legumes feature prominently in the Mediterranean diet and among the so-called 'Blue Zones', where people typically enjoy long, healthy lives. Here, black-eyed beans (mavromatika) make a wonderfully health-giving salad that can be popped into the fridge and enjoyed the next day.

Feeds 4-6

- 250 g (9 oz) dried black-eyed beans
- 3 spring onions (scallions), sliced
- 2 celery stalks, finely diced, plus a few celery heart leaves, torn
- small handful of parsley leaves, finely chopped
- small handful of dill leaves, finely chopped
- 2 tablespoons extra virgin olive oil
- 2 tablespoons white wine vinegar
- salt flakes and freshly cracked black pepper

Rinse the beans well, place in a large saucepan and cover with fresh cold water. Bring to the boil, then cook over medium–low heat for about 1 hour, until the beans are tender. Drain the beans and allow to cool completely.

Place the cooled beans in a large bowl with the spring onion, celery, celery leaves and herbs. Mix to combine.

In a small bowl, whisk together the olive oil and vinegar. Season with salt flakes and cracked pepper.

Toss the dressing through the bean salad.

A NOTE ON PREP
The beans can be boiled the day before and kept covered in the fridge.
The dressing can also be made the day before and stored in a sealed jar.

We also love tinned beans when time is short - two 400 g (14 oz) tins would make a similar amount, simply rinse and drain the beans well before using.

SERVE ME WITH
Plenty of salty olives on the side! We served this salad at a girls' dinner with our Scampi spaghetti with confit tomato (page 93), and it was truly delicious. Make sure you spoon some beans next to your spaghetti.

PATATOSALATA
Herby potato salad

Patatosalata is more than just a salad – it's a testament to the Greek philosophy that food doesn't need to be complicated. Some like to add capers and sweet paprika to theirs, but no matter the variation, the essence of this salad remains the same. We've used dill and parsley, but feel free to use basil and/or coriander (cilantro) instead.

Tossing the dressing through still-warm potatoes is a really important part of this salad, so the dressing coats the potatoes nicely.

In a large bowl, mix together the spring onion, dill, parsley, olive oil and lemon juice. Season with salt flakes and cracked pepper and set aside.

Peel the potatoes and cut into 3 cm (1¼ in) chunks. Place in a saucepan of cold salted water over high heat and bring to the boil. Reduce the heat and simmer for 20 minutes, or until the potatoes are tender, and a sharp knife slips through them easily.

Drain the potatoes and set aside to cool slightly, then transfer to the bowl with the herby oil dressing and stir to combine. You want the potatoes to be slightly warm, so the dressing coats them nicely.

Gently pile the salad onto a serving platter.

Feeds 4

- 2 spring onions (scallions), finely sliced
- ¼ bunch of dill, leaves picked, finely chopped
- ½ bunch of parsley, finely chopped
- 125 ml (½ cup) extra virgin olive oil
- 60 ml (¼ cup) lemon juice
- salt flakes and freshly cracked black pepper
- 1 kg (2 lb 3 oz) all-purpose potatoes

A NOTE ON PREP
If you're short on time the salad can be made the day before. This salad is really delicious the day after it's made as all the herbs will have been marinating with the potatoes. Just make sure to bring the salad to room temperature before serving.

SERVE ME WITH
Our Swordfish with roasted grapes and green olive salsa (page 87).

BEETROOT WITH MIZITHRA CHEESE

Earthy and sweet, beetroot is a vegetable we disliked as kids, but absolutely adore as adults; it really is a wonderful vegetable to cook with. The beetroot can also be boiled for this recipe, but we prefer to roast them, as roasting releases their natural sweetness.

Mizithra cheese can be bought fresh, similar to Italian ricotta, as well as salt-dried, the latter is perfect for grating, and has a mild and slightly tangy flavour that pairs so well with beetroot.

Preheat the oven 200°C (400°F).

Place the beetroot on a piece of foil. Drizzle half the olive oil over them, season with salt flakes and wrap them tightly in the foil. Place on a baking tray and roast for 1 hour, or until a knife slips through them easily. Leave to cool slightly.

In a small bowl, whisk together the remaining olive oil with the vinegar, honey and dried oregano. Season with salt flakes.

Carefully peel the warm beetroot, discarding the skins. Cut into 5 cm (2 in) chunks and place in a large bowl, along with the reserved beetroot leaves, spring onion and parsley. Drizzle the dressing over the salad and gently toss.

Transfer the salad to a serving platter and top with the shaved mizithra cheese.

Feeds 4-6

- 1 kg (2 lb 3 oz) bunch of beetroot (beets), leaves picked, washed and chopped
- 80 ml (⅓ cup) olive oil
- salt flakes
- 1 tablespoon red wine vinegar
- ½ teaspoon honey
- ½ teaspoon dried Greek oregano
- 2 spring onions (scallions), finely sliced
- small handful of parsley leaves, finely chopped
- 60 g (2 oz) salt-dried mizithra cheese, shaved

A NOTE ON PREP
The beetroot can be roasted the day before and stored in a covered container in the fridge.

SERVE ME WITH
Our Pork spare ribs with lemon and oregano on (page 112) and a glass of white wine.

DAKOS SALAD

Barley rusks (paximadi) are a key component of this traditional salad from the island of Crete. The rusks are typically broken into smaller pieces to make them easier to enjoy, their dry, hard texture soaks up all those tomato juices nicely.

Feeds 4-6

- 600 g (1 lb 5 oz) tomatoes
- 60 g (⅓ cup) sun-dried black olives, pitted
- 2 tablespoons baby capers, drained
- 60 ml (¼ cup) extra virgin olive oil
- 1 tablespoon red wine vinegar
- salt flakes and freshly cracked black pepper
- 200 g (7 oz) barley rye rusks, broken into chunks
- 150 g (5½ oz) Greek feta
- 1 teaspoon dried Greek oregano
- small handful of fresh oregano leaves

Grate half the tomatoes and set aside.

Roughly chop the remaining tomatoes and place in a large serving bowl with the olives and capers.

In a small bowl, whisk together the olive oil and vinegar. Season with salt flakes and cracked pepper.

Add the rusk pieces to the serving bowl and toss with the grated tomato and the dressing. Allow the rusks to briefly soak up all the beautiful juices – about 5 minutes should do.

To serve, crumble the feta over the salad and scatter with the dried and fresh oregano.

A NOTE ON PREP
This salad is best prepared fresh, as you don't want the rusks to become too soggy.

SERVE ME WITH
Our Chicken souvlaki with Greek fries (page 106) and a couple of glasses of The Med (page 235).

VEGETABLES

PATATES LEMONATES
Lemon potatoes

Tavernas will often serve their meats or baked dishes with a side of oven-baked potatoes just like these. They're crunchy on the outside, and deliciously soft on the inside. This recipe is so simple, but once you've tried it, we promise you will roast your potatoes like this all the time.

Feeds 4

- 60 ml (¼ cup) extra virgin olive oil
- 3 garlic cloves, crushed
- 60 ml (¼ cup) lemon juice
- 1 teaspoon dried Greek oregano, plus extra to serve
- salt flakes
- 1 kg (2 lb 3 oz) all-purpose potatoes, peeled, cut into thin wedges

Preheat the oven to 200°C (400°F). Grease a large baking tray.

In a large bowl, whisk together the olive oil, garlic, lemon juice and oregano. Season with salt flakes.

Add the potato wedges and toss to coat, then spread them out on the baking tray.

Bake for 50 minutes, turning the wedges over halfway during baking. Bake until the potatoes are golden brown, crispy and fluffy in the middle.

Serve sprinkled with extra dried oregano.

A NOTE ON PREP
The potatoes can be peeled and sliced ahead of time and placed into a bowl of cold water.

SERVE ME WITH
Katsikaki tsigariasto (page 162).

HORTOPITA
Greens pie

In Greece, there are so many variations of 'pitas', from savoury pumpkin (winter squash) pies to hearty chicken-filled pastries. Upon landing in Greece, our first mission is always heading out to find the finest hortopita. Hortopita is a classic Greek pie featuring wild edible greens (horta) and feta cheese tucked inside layers of crispy pastry.

In 2015, we had the privilege of visiting the beautiful town of Florina, seriously the dreamiest town in northern Greece, which is renowned for its vineyards. Eleni, the owner of the beautiful home we stayed at while we were there, shared her secret for making the perfect pita dough. She taught us that vinegar was the key ingredient to help create a crunch to the crust, and she was spot on.

Feeds 6-8

- 250 g (1⅔ cups) plain (all-purpose) flour, sifted, plus extra for dusting
- ½ teaspoon salt flakes
- 1 tablespoon red wine vinegar
- 1 tablespoon extra virgin olive oil, plus extra for brushing
- 220 g (8 oz) English spinach, washed well, then chopped
- small handful of dill leaves, chopped
- small handful of mint leaves, chopped
- 200 g (7 oz) Greek-style yoghurt
- 70 g (2½ oz) Greek feta, crumbled
- freshly cracked black pepper
- lemon wedges, to serve

Preheat the oven to 180°C (350°F).

Place the flour and salt flakes in a large bowl. Make a well in the centre, then pour in the vinegar, olive oil and 100 ml (3½ fl oz) water. Using your hands, slowly bring the dough together to create a ball. Remove from the bowl and knead on a lightly floured work surface for 5 minutes, or until the dough is smooth and elastic.

Place the dough in a large oiled bowl and set aside to rest for 30 minutes.

Blanch the spinach in a saucepan of salted boiling water for 5 minutes, then drain well. When cool enough to handle, squeeze out any excess water, using your hands. Set aside to cool completely.

In a bowl, mix together the cooled spinach, herbs, yoghurt and feta. Season with cracked pepper.

Lightly dust your work surface with extra flour. Remove the dough from the bowl and roll into a 40 cm (15¾ in) round, about 3 mm (⅛ in) thick.

Add the spinach mixture to the centre of the dough, spreading it out evenly, leaving a 6 cm (2½ in) gap from the edges. Fold the edges up around the filling, pleating the dough. Brush the pie with olive oil.

Bake for 45–50 minutes, until the pastry is lightly golden.

Remove from the oven and leave to cool for about 10 minutes before serving with lemon wedges on the side. It is wonderful served warm, but also perfect cold the next day.

A NOTE ON PREP
The dough and filling can both be made the day before and kept covered in the fridge. The following day, use a little flour to dust the dough, then roll out and shape as directed in the recipe.

SERVE ME WITH
Black-eyed bean salad (page 172).

BAMIES
Okra with tomatoes

Our yiayia would usually make bamies at least once a week for an after-school dinner. It wasn't a dish we requested – we would screw up our faces and refuse to eat it. As we got older, we learnt that the way Yiayia cooked hers was not as bad as we thought. Okra is a unique vegetable, and if not cooked the right way it can taste horrible. Soaking the okra in vinegar helps remove some of the characteristic sliminess.

Feeds 4-6

- 500 g (1 lb 2 oz) fresh okra
- 1 tablespoon white vinegar
- 60 ml (¼ cup) olive oil
- 1 white onion, chopped
- 2 teaspoons dried Greek oregano
- 2 garlic cloves, sliced
- salt flakes and freshly cracked black pepper
- 300 g (10½ oz) cherry tomatoes
- 400 g (14 oz) tinned whole peeled tomatoes
- 100 g (3½ oz) Greek feta, crumbled
- crunchy bread, to serve, optional

Place the okra in a large bowl with the vinegar and leave to soak for 1 hour. Drain the okra, then rinse under running water for 2 minutes, to help remove the sliminess.

Heat the olive oil in a large saucepan over medium heat. Fry the onion and dried oregano for 8 minutes, until the onion has softened. Add the garlic and cook for another 2 minutes. Season with salt flakes and cracked pepper, add the okra and saute for a further 10 minutes.

Add the cherry tomatoes, tinned tomatoes and 125 ml (½ cup) water. Cover and simmer for a further 20 minutes, or until the okra is tender.

Serve with the feta and crunchy bread, if desired.

A NOTE ON PREP
This dish is best cooked on the day of serving, but it also tastes delicious eaten the next day!

SERVE ME WITH
Our Horiatiko psomi (page 59) is perfect for soaking up all that oily goodness.

VEGETABLES

TAVERNA DIARIES

TAVERNA OIKONOMOU

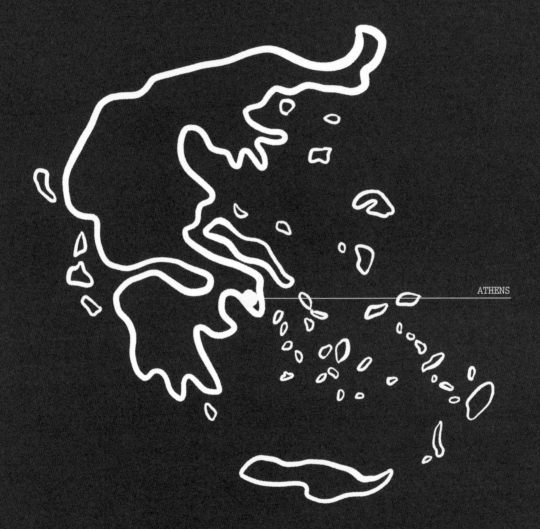

ATHENS

- LOCATION -
Athens

- ADDRESS -
Kidantidon 32 and Troon 41,
Ano Petralona, 11851, Greece

- PHONE -
+30 21 0346 7555

- RECIPE -
Lahanodolmades (Cabbage rolls with avgolemono)

TAVERNA OIKONOMOU is located in the Petralona neighbourhood of Athens, a vibrant, up-and-coming suburb known for its mix of old-world charm and modern energy. Located southwest of the Acropolis, it is divided into two sections: Ano (upper) Petralona, which is more residential and traditional, and Kato (lower) Petralona, where you'll find a growing number of hip cafes, bars and restaurants.

Known for its authentic, home-cooked dishes focused on local produce, and offering a nostalgic taste within an unpretentious space, Taverna Oikonomou really is a special place. The interior is charming and rustic, with simple decor that reflects the taverna's history, which spans nearly a century.

The previous owner, Mr Kostas, ran the taverna for almost 22 years, and wanted to leave it to someone who would love it unconditionally and continue its legacy. The current owner, Vasileios, used to be a regular customer here, and is a man who absolutely loves food and wine and, of course, meeting new people.

'Should we set up the table? Is that one alright?' As soon as we arrive, the staff are already working hard to make us feel at home. Vasileios sits down with us and shares his vision for the taverna for the next 30 years. He wants to foster a creative community where artists inspire and people come to be inspired. 'We try to hold on to tradition,' he says, 'but sometimes it's difficult - the older recipes are simpler, while the bold flavours of the 1980s, for instance, are more complex for those unfamiliar with gastronomy. Yet our goal remains the same: to build a creative, connected community.'

The taverna showcases a very wide selection of artworks and music on a monthly basis. Amazingly, explains Vasileios, both the music and the art are by people who come to dine here. 'They are our friends,' he says. 'We want to educate younger generations not just in traditional food, but in a taste in art and music as well.' What matters most are the details, he explains. Everything has to be intact - well-cooked food, the right wineglasses, tasty oil, and of course fresh bread from a top-notch bakery in Athens called Kora.

> "The interior is charming and rustic, with simple decor that reflects the taverna's history, which spans nearly a century"

At the heart of the kitchen is Garifalia, who has worked here for almost 32 years. Vasileios likes to highlight the kitchen heroes behind the curtains. Garifalia comes out, a warm smile on her face, radiating this amazing energy, and starts telling us how the kitchen usually smashes out 400 dinner services on a busy night - with just her and another cook in the kitchen preparing the food during the day, then three of them serving the meals at night. They really are the backbone of the taverna.

Garifalia started out as a butcher, a craft that helped her become the amazing chef she is now. 'Being a chef requires logic,' she says, 'but my passion is cooking. Making people happy with food is what I love most.' She has full control over the kitchen, creating new recipes and delighting diners with her delicious dishes.

Garifalia's personal favourite is fricassee - a simple yet irresistible stew featuring different combinations of ingredients such as lamb, lettuce, onions and avgolemono (egg and lemon sauce). Another beloved dish is Htapodi me makaronaki kofto (page 90), which is typically enjoyed around Easter.

'Well-cooked food has the power to transport you,' she says, especially when you are with your parea - the people you love. Garifalia's all-time favourite dish to enjoy with her parea is bakaliaro plaki, a baked cod dish from Kalamata. It's the type of food that feels like poetry, like you're feeding your family.

When Garifalia took us on a tour around the kitchen and we saw her lahanodolmades (cabbage rolls) gently steaming away in a big pot on the stove, we just knew this was the recipe we had to share with you!

LAHANODOLMADES
Cabbage rolls with avgolemono

Feeds 4–6; makes about 14 rolls

1 large round cabbage, about 1.2 kg (2 lb 10 oz)
500 g (1 lb 2 oz) minced (ground) beef
120 g (4½ oz) arborio rice
1 egg, lightly beaten
1 brown onion, chopped
small handful of chopped parsley leaves, plus finely chopped stalks
100 ml (3½ fl oz) extra virgin olive oil
1 tablespoon salt flakes, plus extra for seasoning the cooking water
freshly cracked black pepper

AVGOLEMONO
2 egg yolks
60 ml (¼ cup) lemon juice
½ teaspoon cornflour (corn starch)

Carefully cut out the inside core of the cabbage and discard it. Remove the outer leaves and set them aside for lining the bottom of your saucepan.

Fill a large saucepan with water and bring to the boil over medium heat. Place the whole cabbage in the pan, submerging it in the water (you can put a heatproof plate on top to keep it submerged if needed). Boil for 15 minutes, or until the leaves start to come away from the base of the cabbage. Carefully remove the cabbage from the water, reserving the cooking liquid. Gently remove the cabbage leaves one by one, then set them aside to cool slightly.

In a large bowl, combine the beef, rice, egg, onion, half the chopped parsley leaves and stalks and 2 tablespoons of the olive oil. Season with the salt flakes and cracked pepper.

To prepare the cabbage rolls, lay a cabbage leaf on your work surface. Remove any of the bits around the base of the leaf that still seem hard. Place 3 tablespoons (75 g/2¾ oz) of the beef mixture in the bottom centre of the cabbage leaf. Fold the left side of the leaf over to enclose the filling, then fold the right side over to enclose the cabbage. Tightly roll the cabbage from the bottom upwards to finish the roll. Repeat with the remaining cabbage leaves and filling.

Line the bottom of a large saucepan with the reserved outer cabbage leaves. Carefully place the cabbage rolls in the pan, folded side down, layering them side by side so they fit snugly. Pour the remaining olive oil over, scatter with the remaining parsley and season with more salt flakes and cracked pepper. Place an inverted plate on top of the cabbage rolls to hold them down. Pour 750 ml (3 cups) of the reserved cabbage water into the gaps around the plate. Place a lid on top and boil over medium-low heat for 1½ hours, or until the cabbage rolls are tender.

In a bowl, whisk together the avgolemono ingredients for 3–4 minutes, until slightly foamy. Carefully pour the sauce over the cabbage rolls, shaking the pan to make sure the sauce reaches the bottom of the pan. Place the lid back on and simmer for a further 20 minutes, until the avgolemono has become creamy.

Place the cabbage rolls on a serving platter and serve with the delicious lemony avgolemono sauce spooned over. They are equally delicious hot or cold.

<u>A NOTE ON PREP</u>
This recipe requires patience – it's the sort of dish you can make on a Sunday in your PJs with family. You can boil the cabbage leaves ahead of time and also have the filling ready to go.

<u>SERVE ME WITH</u>
Fresh bread and our Horiatiki salata (page 168).

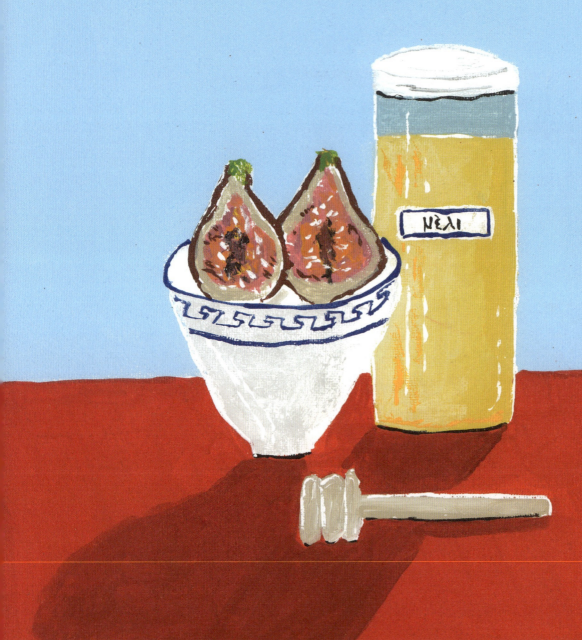

TO FINISH

KEPAΣMA

It's no secret that Greeks are known for their warm hospitality and generosity. This spirit of abundance shines through at the end of every taverna meal with a tradition known as kerasma – a little something on the house. It could be a plate of freshly cut watermelon, a shot of mastiha liqueur, a slice of halva, or a syrup-soaked dessert that's impossible to resist. First-time visitors to Greece are always pleasantly surprised by this, and it's great to see the happy, often amazed, look on their faces. These little touches are what make people fall in love with Greece and keep them coming back.

By the time kerasma arrives, we've usually loosened the top button of our pants, but somehow there's always room for a little something sweet. Growing up, Greek sweets were a staple at the end of every meal at home, with Galaktoboureko (page 200) being a particular favourite of ours.

In this chapter, we share some of Greece's most popular taverna desserts – the ones we can never resist.

A TREAT TO FINISH

JAMMY FIGS WITH HONEY & YOGHURT
196

LOUKOUMADES
Honey puffs with pistachio
199

GALAKTOBOUREKO WITH WALNUTS
Milk custard pie
200

MOSAIKO
Greek chocolate slice
202

YIAOURTOPITA
Lemon yoghurt cake
205

LADOKOULOURA
Olive oil and orange biscuits
206

KARIDOPITA
Walnut syrup cake
208

SPICED ALMOND & PISTACHIO KATAIFI
211

DARK CHOCOLATE-COATED
ALMOND CLUSTERS
212

SOUR CHERRY & VERMOUTH GRANITA
215

OUZO & CITRUS SORBET
216

STICKY FIG & HONEY SEMIFREDDO
219

GLYKO TOU KOUTALIOU
Grape spoon sweet
220

JAMMY FIGS WITH HONEY & YOGHURT

We photographed this recipe in a beautiful village called Margarites, which is near the town of Rethymno in Crete. The figs were picked fresh that morning and were perfectly jammy inside, and we served them with a local goat's milk yoghurt, which is a staple in the Cretan diet, and the best local honey we could find. Goat's milk yoghurt has a light texture and is rich in flavour, it's worth seeking out but if you can't find it you can use cow's milk yoghurt instead.

Spoon the yoghurt onto a serving plate and top with the figs. Drizzle with honey and serve.

Enjoy in the sunshine.

Feeds 4

600 g (1 lb 5 oz) thick goat's milk yoghurt
6 figs, halved
90 g (3 oz) Greek honey

A NOTE ON PREP
This is best prepared when ready to serve.

SERVE ME WITH
A small handful of roasted chopped walnuts.

OPA!

LOUKOUMADES
Honey puffs with pistachio

Back in the 1990s, the Greek festival in Adelaide would happen once a year, and we would always look forward to ordering loukoumades with plenty of honey and a good dusting of cinnamon on top. Something about the way they were prepared always made us want more. Deep-fried, crispy and golden on the outside, loukoumades are best made fresh to order.

Feeds 6-8

- 7 g sachet (2¼ teaspoons) active dried yeast
- 1 tablespoon caster (superfine) sugar
- 600 g (4 cups) plain (all-purpose) flour, sifted
- ½ teaspoon fine sea salt
- 1 teaspoon ouzo (optional)
- vegetable oil, for deep-frying
- 350 g (1 cup) honey
- 100 g (⅔ cup) pistachios, finely chopped, plus extra to serve
- ground cinnamon, for sprinkling

Pour 750 ml (3 cups) warm water into a jug. Add the yeast and sugar and whisk to combine. Set aside for 10 minutes, or until frothy.

Place the flour and salt in a large bowl. Make a well in the centre, pour in the yeast mixture, and the ouzo, if using, and whisk until smooth. Cover with a damp tea towel, then leave to stand for 1 hour, or until the dough has doubled in size.

Half-fill a saucepan with vegetable oil and heat to 180°C (350°F) on a kitchen thermometer.

Working in batches, drop heaped tablespoons of the batter into the oil and cook for 6–7 minutes, until golden brown, turning the loukoumades over every now and then. Drain on paper towel to absorb any excess oil.

Put the honey, pistachios and 1 tablespoon boiling water in a large bowl and stir to combine. Toss the loukoumades in the honey mixture and coat well.

Serve immediately, with a sprinkling of cinnamon and the extra chopped pistachios.

A NOTE ON PREP
Unfortunately, the batter can't be prepared ahead of time, and needs to be cooked and served as the recipe directs.

SERVE ME WITH
A freddo cappuccino, preferably in the sun.

GALAKTOBOUREKO WITH WALNUTS
Milk custard pie

A milk custard pie with crispy, buttery layers of filo pastry, drenched in a lemon syrup – just the thought has us drooling. This is the dessert we wait all year to eat. The second we arrive in Greece we'll buy one (thankfully they are sold on nearly every street corner). Our version isn't quite traditional, as we have added roasted walnuts to the base, but they really do add a beautiful flavour.

Feeds 8-10

- 1.5 litres (6 cups) full-cream (whole) milk
- 115 g (½ cup) caster (superfine) sugar
- 1 vanilla bean, split lengthways, seeds scraped
- 180 g (6½ oz) fine semolina
- 4 eggs, lightly beaten
- 150 g (5½ oz) unsalted butter, melted
- 375 g (13 oz) fresh filo pastry
- 200 g (7 oz) walnuts, roasted and finely chopped

LEMON SYRUP
- 220 g (8 oz) caster (superfine) sugar
- zest of 2 small lemons, plus 2 tablespoons lemon juice
- 210 ml (7 fl oz) water

Place the milk, sugar, vanilla bean and vanilla seeds in a saucepan and bring to a simmer over medium heat. Remove the vanilla bean and whisk in the semolina in a steady stream. While whisking, slowly pour in the beaten egg, then reduce the heat to medium–low and continue whisking for about 20 minutes, until you have a thick custard that coats the back of a spoon.

Remove the saucepan from the heat and allow to cool slightly, then cover the surface of the custard with plastic wrap to prevent a skin forming. Set aside.

Set out a 26 cm (10¼ in) round baking dish that's at least 5 cm (2 in) deep. Brush the base with some of the melted butter, then top with one sheet of filo pastry. Repeat with another nine pastry sheets, alternating them lengthways and crossways, and brushing each layer with butter. Evenly scatter the walnuts over the top layer of pastry. Pour the custard over the walnuts and leave to sit for 10 minutes.

Meanwhile, preheat the oven to 180°C (350°F).

Repeat the filo layering and buttering process with another six pastry sheets to cover the custard. (Any leftover pastry can be wrapped tightly and stored in the fridge for another use.) Then, using a sharp knife, carefully score the top of the pastry into eight slices. Tuck in any overhanging pastry around the edges. Transfer to the oven and bake for 50 minutes, or until the pastry is golden and crisp.

To make the lemon syrup, place all the syrup ingredients in a small saucepan over medium–high heat and bring to the boil. Reduce the heat to medium–low and simmer for 10 minutes, or until the syrup becomes thick. Set aside to cool slightly.

Pour the warm lemon syrup over the hot galaktoboureko and allow to stand for 15 minutes. Serve warm, or at room temperature.

A NOTE ON PREP
The entire dish can be made up to 5 days ahead, right up until the step where it goes into the oven; just be sure to coat the top of the pastry with melted butter, so it doesn't dry out, then cover with plastic wrap and store in the fridge. When you're ready to bake the pie, remove it from the fridge and bring to room temperature before placing it in a preheated oven.

SERVE ME WITH
A Greek coffee (page 230).

A TREAT TO FINISH

MOSAIKO
Greek chocolate slice

Every country has its own version of mosaiko, and this is how the Greeks make it. In our cookbook *Peinão*, we included a mosaiko recipe that featured walnuts and sour cherries, and we had to include another version here again as it's such a popular sweet to finish the night on. Usually, nuts are added into the mix, but we have kept this version simple. Brandy is optional, but really complements the chocolate.

This is truly one of the easiest desserts to make, and you can prepare it well in advance.

Line a 10 cm × 25 cm (4 in × 10 in) loaf (bar) tin with baking paper.

Melt the butter in a saucepan over low heat. Add the condensed milk, chocolate and cocoa powder and mix until melted and well combined. Stir in the brandy or milk.

Break the biscuits into roughly 2 cm (¾ in) pieces, and transfer to a large bowl. Pour the chocolate mixture over and gently mix until the biscuit pieces are well coated.

Spoon the mixture into the loaf tin and use a spoon to flatten the top. Cover with baking paper and leave to set in the fridge overnight.

The following day, remove the baking paper and cut the mosaiko into 2 cm (¾ in) thick slices. Serve dusted with extra cocoa powder.

Makes 12

- 160 g (5½ oz) unsalted butter, chopped
- 397 g (14 oz) tinned condensed milk
- 220 g (8 oz) good-quality dark chocolate, chopped
- 60 g (½ cup) Dutch cocoa powder, sifted, plus extra for dusting
- 2 teaspoons brandy or full-cream (whole) milk
- 225 g (8 oz) plain sweet biscuits, such as Marie biscuits

A NOTE ON PREP
You will need to make this the day before and leave it in the fridge overnight. The mosaiko will keep in an airtight container in the fridge for up to 10 days.

SERVE ME WITH
Usually mosaiko is enjoyed on its own, alongside a cup of coffee or hot mountain tea.

YIAOURTOPITA
Lemon yoghurt cake

On days when we feel like something sweet, we tend to bake a yiaourtopita. The yoghurt gives the cake a moist and fluffy texture, while the lemon adds a lovely tang.

In winter, when oranges and mandarins are in season and so juicy and sweet, we love to use them in this cake instead of lemons.

Feeds 6-8

180 g (6½ oz) unsalted butter, softened, plus extra for greasing
180 g (6½ oz) caster (superfine) sugar
4 large eggs, separated
zest of 1 large lemon
60 ml (¼ cup) lemon juice
1 teaspoon vanilla bean extract
200 g (7 oz) Greek-style yoghurt, plus extra to serve
250 g (1⅔ cups) self-raising flour, sifted
½ teaspoon baking powder

LEMON SYRUP
230 g (1 cup) caster (superfine) sugar
zest of 1 lemon
60 ml (¼ cup) lemon juice
60 ml (¼ cup) water

Place all the lemon syrup ingredients in a small saucepan over medium heat. Bring to a simmer, stirring often, then continue to simmer for 7–8 minutes, until thickened and syrupy. Remove from the heat and set aside to cool.

Preheat the oven to 180°C (350°F). Grease the base and side of a 20 cm (8 in) round or square cake tin.

Place the butter and sugar in the bowl of a stand mixer fitted with the paddle attachment. Beat until light and creamy, then add the egg yolks and beat until combined.

Fold the lemon zest, lemon juice, vanilla and yoghurt through, using a large metal spoon. In a bowl, combine the flour and baking powder, then add to the yoghurt mixture and gently fold to combine.

Using a clean bowl and a stand mixer fitted with the whisk attachment, whisk the egg whites until stiff peaks form. Gently fold the egg white through the yoghurt mixture, using a large clean metal spoon.

Pour the batter into the baking tin and bake for 45 minutes, or until the cake is golden and a skewer inserted in the centre comes out clean.

Remove the cake from the oven, leaving it in the tin. Poke skewer holes into the cake. Evenly pour the cooled lemon syrup over, then leave to soak in for 1 hour.

Turn the cake out of the tin. Slice and serve with an extra dollop of yoghurt.

A NOTE ON PREP
The cake can be baked ahead of time and stored in an airtight container. It will keep at room temperature for 2 days, and 5-7 days in the fridge.

SERVE ME WITH
The perfect Greek coffee (page 230).

LADOKOULOURA
Olive oil and orange biscuits

There are a bunch of Greek products we always pack in our suitcases to bring back to Australia when departing Greece. This is one of them. 'Ladokouloura' translates as 'olive oil cookies', and are mostly eaten during Lent. Made using good-quality olive oil, ground cinnamon and cloves and freshly squeezed orange juice, they are the perfect dipping biscuit for Greek coffee, especially in the morning, as these cookies are not too sweet.

We use light olive oil instead of extra virgin olive oil here, otherwise the flavour can be overpowering.

Preheat the oven to 180°C (350°F). Line two large baking trays with baking paper.

In a large bowl, combine the flour, baking powder, cinnamon, cloves and sugar. Make a well in the centre, then mix in the olive oil, orange zest and orange juice until combined.

Roll a heaped tablespoon of the mixture into a 10–11 cm (4–4¼ in) long rope and gently press both ends together to form a ring. Place on a baking tray and repeat with the remaining dough. Gently brush the cookies with water, then sprinkle with the sesame seeds.

Bake for 18–20 minutes, until the cookies are lightly golden. Remove from the oven and allow to cool completely.

Makes about 20

- 300 g (2 cups) plain (all-purpose) flour, sifted
- 1 teaspoon baking powder
- 1 teaspoon ground cinnamon
- ½ teaspoon ground cloves
- 80 g (⅓ cup) caster (superfine) sugar
- 100 ml (3½ fl oz) good-quality light olive oil
- zest of 1 small orange
- 100 ml (3½ fl oz) orange juice
- 2 tablespoons sesame seeds

A NOTE ON PREP
The biscuits can be made the day before serving and will keep in a large airtight container in the pantry for 5-7 days.

SERVE ME WITH
A cup of Greek coffee (page 230) or a Frappe (page 232).

KARIDOPITA
Walnut syrup cake

This fluffy cake made from crushed roasted walnuts, which is soaked in a sweet honey and orange syrup, is the perfect bite to finish any evening meal. In Thessaloniki, in the suburb of Panorama where our family lives, there is a dessert shop that sells a very delicious karidopita. It's always been our favourite shop to buy a couple of desserts to take back to our aunt's house to eat while we listen to Greek music and spend quality family time together.

There are several variations of this cake. Some recipes use flour, but fine breadcrumbs are more traditional. This cake is best eaten chilled, allowing the cake to sit in the fridge overnight so all the syrup really soaks in is ideal.

Feeds 8-10

- 400 g (14 oz) walnuts
- 200 g (7 oz) unsalted butter, softened, plus extra for greasing
- 150 g (5½ oz) caster (superfine) sugar
- 7 large eggs, separated
- zest of 1 small orange
- 2 teaspoons brandy or orange juice
- 140 g (5 oz) shop-bought fine breadcrumbs
- 1 tablespoon baking powder
- 1 tablespoon ground cinnamon
- ½ teaspoon ground cloves
- ½ teaspoon freshly grated nutmeg

HONEY & ORANGE SYRUP
- 460 g (2 cups) caster (superfine) sugar
- 100 g (3½ oz) honey
- 2 tablespoons orange juice
- 1 cinnamon stick
- 500 ml (2 cups) water

Preheat the oven to 180°C (350°F).

Finely chop 2 tablespoons of the walnuts and set aside for sprinkling over the top of the finished cake.

Place the remaining walnuts on a baking tray and roast for 8–10 minutes, until lightly golden. Allow the walnuts to cool, then chop finely using a sharp knife.

Using an electric mixer, beat the butter and sugar for 5 minutes, until smooth and creamy. Add the egg yolks, one at a time, until well combined. Stir the orange zest and brandy through. Fold the walnuts, breadcrumbs, baking powder and spices through the butter mixture. Note that the mixture will be slightly solid; don't panic, this is fine.

Turn the oven down to 170°C (340°F). Grease a 20 cm × 30 cm (8 in × 12 in) rectangular cake tin – one that's at least 6 cm (2½) in deep – with the extra butter.

Using a clean bowl and beaters, whisk the egg whites until stiff peaks form. Using a large metal spoon, gradually fold the beaten egg white through the walnut mixture until smooth.

Spoon the mixture into the cake tin and bake for 30–35 minutes, until the cake is lightly golden. Remove from the oven and allow the cake to cool slightly.

While the cake is cooling, place all the syrup ingredients in a saucepan over medium heat. Simmer for 5–7 minutes, until thickened and syrupy. Pour the hot syrup over the cooled cake and leave to absorb. Allow the cake to cool completely, ideally in the fridge overnight, before serving.

Slice the cake into diamond shapes and scatter with the reserved chopped walnuts.

A NOTE ON PREP
Prepare this cake the day before you want to serve it. It will keep covered in the fridge for up to 1 week.

Use a sharp knife to chop the walnuts, avoid using a food processor as it will make the walnuts too powdery.

SERVE ME WITH
A dollop of Greek-style yoghurt would be lovely to cut through the sweetness. Or, for something a little different, crumble the karidopita over some vanilla ice cream.

Spiced Almond & Pistachio Kataifi

Kataifi is such a popular dessert in Greece and the Middle East, and each country has its own way of making it – but it all starts with kataifi pastry, a thread-like pastry. To make it, a crepe-like batter that is dripped onto a rotating heated metal plate through fine spouts, where it is briefly dried and cooked. You'll find kataifi pastry at your local European or Greek deli, in the fridge or freezer. The pastry needs to be thawed completely to room temperature before opening the packet, so it is soft and pliable. To stop it going dry, drape a damp tea towel over the pastry when you're not using it.

Our yiayia would always say, 'cold syrup over hot kataifi' – great advice, because if you put hot syrup on hot kataifi, the heat can make the pastry go mushy, and if you put cold syrup on cold kataifi, the syrup will not absorb all the way through.

Makes 21

- 100 g (⅔ cup) unsalted pistachios
- 100 g (⅔ cup) almonds
- 300 g (10½ oz) unsalted butter, melted, plus extra for greasing
- 1 teaspoon ground cinnamon
- ¼ teaspoon freshly grated nutmeg
- ¼ teaspoon ground cloves
- 1 tablespoon caster (superfine) sugar
- 375 g (13 oz) packet of kataifi pastry (shredded pastry)

SYRUP
- 460 g (2 cups) caster (superfine) sugar
- peeled zest of 1 lemon
- 1 cinnamon stick
- 250 ml (1 cup) water

Preheat the oven to 170°C (340°F). Spread the pistachios and almonds on a baking tray and roast in the oven for 5–7 minutes, until lightly browned. Remove from the oven and set aside to cool.

Turn the oven temperature up to 180°C (350°F). Grease the base and sides of a 20 cm × 25 cm (8 in × 10 in) rectangular baking dish with melted butter.

Combine the syrup ingredients in a small saucepan over high heat. Bring to a simmer, then reduce the heat to medium and cook, stirring occasionally, for 8–10 minutes, until the sugar has dissolved and the liquid has reduced slightly. Set aside to cool.

In a food processor, whiz the roasted pistachios and almonds until the nuts are finely chopped. Place them in a bowl, along with the cinnamon, nutmeg, cloves and sugar, and stir to combine.

Unroll the kataifi pastry and, using your hands, gently separate the pastry. Be careful when handling kataifi – it is very fragile. Tear off a piece of kataifi, about 4 cm (1½ in) wide and 16 cm (6¼ in) long. Brush it with melted butter and place 1 tablespoon of the nut filling on top, along the short edge. Roll the pastry tightly to form a cylinder. Place in the baking dish and repeat with the remaining pastry and filling.

Brush the kataifi with the remaining melted butter, then bake for 45 minutes, or until the pastry is lightly golden brown. Remove the dish from the oven and evenly pour the cold syrup over the hot kataifi. Set aside until cooled to room temperature, and all the syrup has been absorbed.

A NOTE ON PREP
This dessert can be made ahead, ready to bring out when people arrive. It will keep for up to 5 days in an airtight container in the pantry.

SERVE ME WITH
Our Frappe (page 232) or a hot cup of chamomile tea.

DARK CHOCOLATE-COATED ALMOND CLUSTERS

This sweet snack is quite nostalgic for us. Our mum's aunt Aleka would offer these each time we visited her in her village on the Kassandra peninsula in Halkidiki, presenting them in a small basket covered in foil.

In the main cities of Greece, you'll find a sweets shop in almost every suburb, and there'll be a section where you can order chocolate-coated nuts – like these clusters – by the kilo, made with either milk chocolate or dark chocolate, and sometimes other nuts. When travelling through Greece, we always make sure we order a bag for the road.

Makes about 26

400 g (14 oz) almonds
400 g (14 oz) dark chocolate (70% cocoa solids), melted
salt flakes, for sprinkling

Preheat the oven to 180°C (350°F).

Place the almonds on a baking tray and roast on the middle shelf of the oven for 15 minutes, or until they are lightly golden and smell fragrant. Remove from the oven and set aside to cool for 10 minutes.

Line another baking tray with baking paper, making sure the baking tray fits into your fridge.

Place the melted chocolate in a bowl and stir the almonds through until well coated. Leave to sit for about 20 minutes, or until the mixture is slightly thick. (This makes it easier to spoon the mixture onto the tray.)

Spoon tablespoons of the chocolate almond mixture onto the lined baking tray, making sure to stack them into small clusters. Sprinkle with sea salt flakes.

Place the almond clusters in the fridge for 6 hours or overnight, or until the chocolate has hardened.

A NOTE ON PREP
We usually have a batch of these in the fridge to enjoy as a midweek sweet. They will keep in an airtight container for up to 2 weeks.

SERVE ME WITH
A cup of freshly brewed Greek coffee (page 230) or Greek mountain tea.

SOUR CHERRY & VERMOUTH GRANITA

This dish is inspired by a cocktail we had in Greece one summer, and as soon as we drank it we knew we had to turn it into a granita. Sour cherries, known as 'vissino' in Greek, hold a special place in Greek sweets and desserts. You'll find sour cherry products in specialty food stores.

Feeds 4–6

- 55 g (¼ cup) caster (superfine) sugar
- 60 ml (¼ cup) lemon juice
- 2 tablespoons sour cherry syrup
- 500 ml (2 cups) sour cherry juice
- 80 ml (⅓ cup) sweet vermouth

Place the sugar, lemon juice, sour cherry syrup and 250 ml (1 cup) of the sour cherry juice in a small saucepan. Simmer over medium heat for 5–6 minutes, until the sugar has dissolved. Add the remaining 250 ml (1 cup) sour cherry juice and allow the mixture to cool completely.

Once cooled, stir in the sweet vermouth and pour the mixture into a 16 cm × 25 cm (6¼ in × 10 in) tray that's at least 5 cm (2 in) deep. Place in the freezer for 1 hour.

Use a fork to scrape the mixture from the edges of the tray into the centre, then spread out again. Return to the freezer for 30 minutes and repeat the process until the granita is completely frozen into a sandy texture of ice crystals.

To serve, simply scoop the granita into glasses.

A NOTE ON PREP
The granita needs to be made at least a day ahead of serving. It will keep covered in the freezer for up to 1 week.

SERVE ME WITH
Perfect enjoyed on its own and on a warm summer's day with good company.

OUZO & CITRUS SORBET

Feeds 4

320 g (11½ oz) caster (superfine) sugar
300 ml (10 fl oz) freshly squeezed mandarin juice (from about 8 mandarins)
300 ml (10 fl oz) freshly squeezed orange juice
80 ml (⅓ cup) ouzo

We tested this recipe with a bunch of friends who were there to sample it – and finally, after a couple of tests, everyone loved it. We won't be surprised if this recipe becomes your favourite sorbet, as it is sure to be an instant hit with your friends! The fresh citrus juice cuts through the strong ouzo flavour and is perfect for a hot day.

Place the sugar and 400 ml (13½ fl oz) water in a small saucepan over medium–low heat. Bring to the boil, stirring continuously for 2 minutes, or until the sugar has dissolved. Allow to cool completely.

Stir in the mandarin juice, orange juice and ouzo until combined. Pour the mixture into an ice-cream machine and churn for 1½ hours, or until creamy.

Spoon the sorbet into a plastic container and place in the freezer for 5 hours or overnight to harden.

Serve scooped into bowls.

A NOTE ON PREP
The sorbet needs to be made at least a day ahead of serving. It will keep covered in the freezer for up to 1 week.

SERVE ME WITH
Sunshine! It is also the perfect dessert if you're after something refreshing after a big meal.

STICKY FIG & HONEY SEMIFREDDO

We grew up with a fig tree in our garden and one at our yiayia and papou's house in Adelaide, so we know how figs should taste. Growing up, we would use our papou's painting ladder to pick the figs, and they are still the most beautiful figs we have ever had. Even to this day we can't find better figs.

Greece is home to several varieties of figs, with most households having a fig tree in their garden. The fruit is often shared among neighbours and family. Whether fresh or dried, figs are an essential part of the Greek culinary experience – especially in summer when they are ripe and ready to be eaten straight off the tree.

Here, sweet jammy figs star in our semifreddo – which is one of those fabulous desserts that you can make ahead and have ready to go when guests arrive.

Serves 4

6 figs, stems removed, roughly chopped
230 g (1 cup) caster (superfine) sugar
500 ml (2 cups) cream
1 teaspoon vanilla bean paste
4 egg yolks
Greek honey, to serve

Place the figs and half the sugar in a small saucepan over low heat. Cook for 15 minutes, or until the figs are softened and jammy, stirring occasionally. Scoop the figs and syrup into a bowl, then leave in the fridge for 15 minutes to cool completely.

Line a loaf (bar) tin with plastic wrap. Ideally, the tin would measure 9.5 cm × 20 cm (3¾ in × 8 in) around the base, and 11.5 cm × 23 cm (4½ in × 9 in) around the top.

Pour the cream into a large mixing bowl. Add the vanilla bean paste. Using an electric mixer, lightly whip the cream until soft peaks begin to form.

In a separate bowl, and using clean beaters, whisk the egg yolks and remaining sugar until light and creamy. Add the cream mixture and whisk until combined and creamy.

Pour into the loaf tin and stir the jammy figs through. Cover with plastic wrap and place in the freezer for about 3 hours, until firm.

Once frozen, cut the semifreddo into thick slices and serve drizzled with honey.

A NOTE ON PREP
The joy of this dessert is that it can be prepared the day before and will keep in the freezer for up to 5 days.

SERVE ME WITH
A cold Frappe (page 232).

GLYKO TOU KOUTALIOU
Grape spoon sweet

In Greek culture, sweet fruit preserves are a cherished tradition, created by cooking fruits such as grapes, figs, cherries, oranges, lemons, quinces and sometimes tomatoes in a sugar syrup to retain the fruit's original shape, rather than getting lost in a mash, as with many jams.

These sweet fruit preserves are traditionally served with a small spoon, hence their name – with 'glyko' meaning 'sweet', and 'koutaliou' meaning 'spoon'. In summer, these sweet fruit preserves are often offered to guests after a meal as a gesture of hospitality.

This sweet reminds us of Mum's cousin Eleni, as her kitchen bench always has an array of different spoon sweets in jars, all made with seasonal fruits. We have used white grapes here, but red and black grapes will also work nicely.

Makes 500 g (2 cups)

500 g (1 lb 2 oz) small and medium-sized white grapes, washed
300 g (10½ oz) caster (superfine) sugar
zest of 1 small lemon
100 ml (3½ fl oz) lemon juice
100 ml (3½ fl oz) water

Place all the ingredients in a saucepan over high heat and bring to the boil.

Reduce the heat to low and simmer for 1–1¼ hours, until the grapes have turned a light orange colour, and the mixture turns jammy and becomes slightly thick.

Pour the mixture into a heatproof glass bowl and stir in 1 tablespoon water. Allow to cool completely in the fridge overnight, then pour into a sterilised jar and seal with a lid.

A NOTE ON PREP
This needs to be made at least a day before serving and left in the fridge to cool overnight. It will keep in the fridge for up to 6 months, as long as the grapes are covered with the syrup.

SERVE ME WITH
Sweet fruit preserves are usually served on their own - or on top of some thick Greek-style yoghurt is perfect.

TO US

ΣΤΗΝ ΥΓΕΙΑ ΜΑΣ

OPA!

In Greece, the drinking culture is all about getting together with your parea – group of friends – and enjoying good times, which often stretch late into the night.

At a taverna, you'll typically find a mix of local spirits such as tsipouro and ouzo, bottles of Greek beer poured into small glasses, and chilled house wine, served in either a tetarto (250 ml/8½ fl oz) or miso kilo (500 ml/17 fl oz) carafe.

Whether it's sipping ouzo with your meal, having mojitos on the beach, or kicking off the day with a cold Frappe (page 232), we've put together a collection of drinks that bring back the flavours and vibes of our time in Greece.

These drinks are more than just something to sip – they're a reflection of the memories and moments we've loved during our travels.

CHEERS TO US

TAVERNA DIARIES:
JAZZMIN, AMORGOS -
THE PERFECT GREEK COFFEE
226

FRAPPE
232

THE MED
235

OUZO & OLIVE OIL SOUR
236

POMEGRANATE & MINT SPRITZ
238

TAVERNA DIARIES:
T'APANEMO AMORGOS, AMORGOS -
PSIMENI RAKI
240

TAVERNA DIARIES

JAZZMIN

AMORGOS

- LOCATION -
Amorgos

- ADDRESS -
Chora 840 08, Greece

- PHONE -
+30 2285 074017

- RECIPE -
The perfect Greek coffee

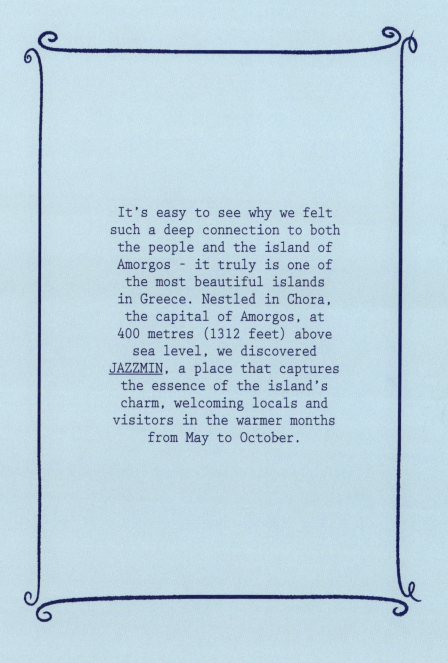

It's easy to see why we felt such a deep connection to both the people and the island of Amorgos - it truly is one of the most beautiful islands in Greece. Nestled in Chora, the capital of Amorgos, at 400 metres (1312 feet) above sea level, we discovered JAZZMIN, a place that captures the essence of the island's charm, welcoming locals and visitors in the warmer months from May to October.

By day, it's a cosy cafe with a bohemian energy; by night, it transforms into a lively bar. For over 20 years, Theodoros Nikolaou Thanos has been the heart and soul of Jazzmin, crafting some of the finest Greek coffee on the island. His warmth and hospitality are as memorable as the coffee itself.

Shaded by bougainvillea vines, the rooftop outdoor seating offers a view of Chora's whitewashed alleys. Mornings here often begin with a breakfast of fried eggs with the brightest yellow yolks, fresh local feta, bread from the local bakery and ripe juicy tomatoes. They bake their own cakes in-house, and there's always something sweet to finish.

As we were leaving Jazzmin, we sat at the bar and chatted with Theodoros, who was more than happy for us to come back and photograph the coffee he has mastered the skill of making. Our yiayia had taught us how to make Greek coffee, but it's such a beautiful process, and everyone loves to share their tips.

Made with finely ground coffee beans, traditional Greek coffee is brewed slowly in a special copper pot known as a briki – before being sipped and enjoyed slowly as part of a cherished ritual that has been around for centuries. (We can still remember the smell of coffee brewing on the stovetop with Yiayia chatting away with her friends as she and Papou made cups of Greek coffee for friends or neighbours who had popped over.)

"By day, it's a cosy cafe with a bohemian energy; by night, it transforms into a lively bar"

Theodoros is passionate about coffee, and uses two blends of Greek coffee - one with cardamom, and one with ground mastiha, which comes from the dried resin of the mastic tree that grows throughout the Mediterranean region. Known as 'tears of Chios' due to the shape of the resin droplets, and the place it was traditionally produced, the mastiha used at Jazzmin has notes of earthy pine and wild herbs, and does indeed come from the island of Chios, located in the north-eastern Aegean Sea near Turkey - an island rich in history, Greek traditions and hospitality.

This is the place to drink a Greek coffee, and maybe play a game of tavli (the national board game, similar to backgammon), or settle back and relax with a book from the selection on display.

Failing that, here's how you can make the perfect Greek coffee at home.

THE PERFECT GREEK COFFEE

Makes 2 small espresso cups

2 tablespoons Greek coffee grounds
2 teaspoons caster (superfine) sugar

Spoon the coffee grounds and sugar into a briki. Add 2 espresso cups worth of water and place over medium heat. Do not stir.

Once the coffee starts to bubble, remove from the heat. A thick foam known as 'kaimaki' should start to form on top, which adds a creamy texture to the coffee.

Carefully pour into two small espresso cups and enjoy.

A NOTE ON PREP
You'll only be able to make two little espresso cups of coffee at a time in a briki, as the pot is so small.

SERVE ME WITH
Ladokouloura (page 206) to dunk straight into the coffee.

FRAPPE

Makes 2

2 teaspoons instant coffee granules, such as Nescafé
1 teaspoon sugar (optional)
2 tablespoons cold water
ice cubes
chilled full-cream (whole) milk or iced water, to serve

Coffee is a big part of Greek culture, and the locals are known to sip away at a single coffee over a few hours. While the coffee of choice these days in Greece is a freddo espresso, we love the nostalgia of an old-school frappe, especially when enjoyed alongside a hot, creamy bougatsa (custard pie).

Place the instant coffee, sugar, if using, and cold water in a milkshake machine or an electric milk frother. Blend for 1–2 minutes, until a foam forms and it becomes light brown.

Pour into two tall glasses, add some ice cubes and top with milk or iced water. Serve cold.

SERVE ME WITH
Ladokouloura (page 206).

THE MED

This cocktail was crafted by our friend Paschalis, to highlight the unique flavours of Skinos Mastiha Spirit, for which he is a global ambassador. This liqueur is derived from the mastic trees of Chios, also known as 'Mastic Island'.

For this recipe we use a simple sugar syrup, made by stirring one part sugar with one part boiling water until dissolved. For a non-alcoholic version, substitute the mastiha for sparkling water. Mandarin juice also works beautifully instead of orange juice.

Makes 2

small handful of basil leaves, plus extra to serve
100 ml (3½ fl oz) mastiha, such as Skinos Mastiha Spirit
1 teaspoon simple sugar syrup (see introduction)
ice cubes
125 ml (½ cup) freshly squeezed orange juice
sparkling water, for topping
1-2 orange slices, halved

Place the basil leaves in a cocktail shaker, along with the mastiha, sugar syrup and a handful of ice cubes. Shake vigorously for 15–20 seconds.

Strain into two highball glasses filled with ice cubes. Top with the orange juice and a splash of sparkling water. Garnish with orange slices and extra basil leaves and serve.

SERVE ME WITH
Once you try this, it will seriously become one of your favourite drinks. Serve alongside Fried whitebait with ouzo mayonnaise (page 66), Patatosalata (page 174) and Octopus with caperberries and lemon (page 68).

OUZO & OLIVE OIL SOUR

Makes 4-6

125 ml (½ cup) ouzo
80 ml (⅓ cup) freshly squeezed
  lemon juice
1 tablespoon sugar syrup
  (see introduction, page 235)
ice cubes
extra virgin olive oil, to
  garnish
a few small fresh lemon thyme
  sprigs, to garnish

Ouzo isn't just a drink, it's a symbol of gratitude and hospitality, and plays such a big role in Greek social gatherings. When you eat at a taverna, it's very common for the waiter to offer you a complimentary shot of ouzo to say thank you for dining at their establishment. It definitely is a distinctive drink, with strong anise notes; some love it … others, not so much. It needs to be enjoyed slowly, each sip revealing layers of its anise flavour.

This really is the perfect drink for a warm day. The olive oil softens the ouzo – and as the ice gently melts away, the sharpness of the ouzo also starts to mellow.

Pour the ouzo, lemon juice and sugar syrup into a cocktail shaker. Add a few ice cubes and shake vigorously for 15–20 seconds, or until frosted on the outside.

Strain into small cocktail glasses. Garnish each drink with 3 drops of olive oil and a lemon thyme sprig and serve.

SERVE ME WITH
Dishes with simple flavours, to complement the ouzo, such as Scampi spaghetti with confit tomato (page 93) and some Stuffed fried olives (page 45).

POMEGRANATE & MINT SPRITZ

Our aunty who lives in Thessaloniki has a pomegranate tree right outside her bedroom window. Each summer we witness the growth of the pomegranates – and if we are lucky enough to come back in winter, the pomegranates are completely grown and ready to eat. We love the crunch of the arils in this cocktail and the freshness from the mint.

Place a couple of ice cubes in two tall glasses.

Pour the gin and pomegranate juice over the ice cubes. Top with the pomegranate seeds and mint leaves, then top with the chilled prosecco and serve.

Makes 2

ice cubes
60 ml (¼ cup) gin
100 ml (3½ fl oz) pomegranate juice
2 tablespoons pomegranate seeds
handful of mint leaves, smashed
chilled prosecco, for topping

SERVE ME WITH
Revithokeftedes (page 42) and King prawns with fennel and caper butter (page 72) for a little outdoor summer feast.

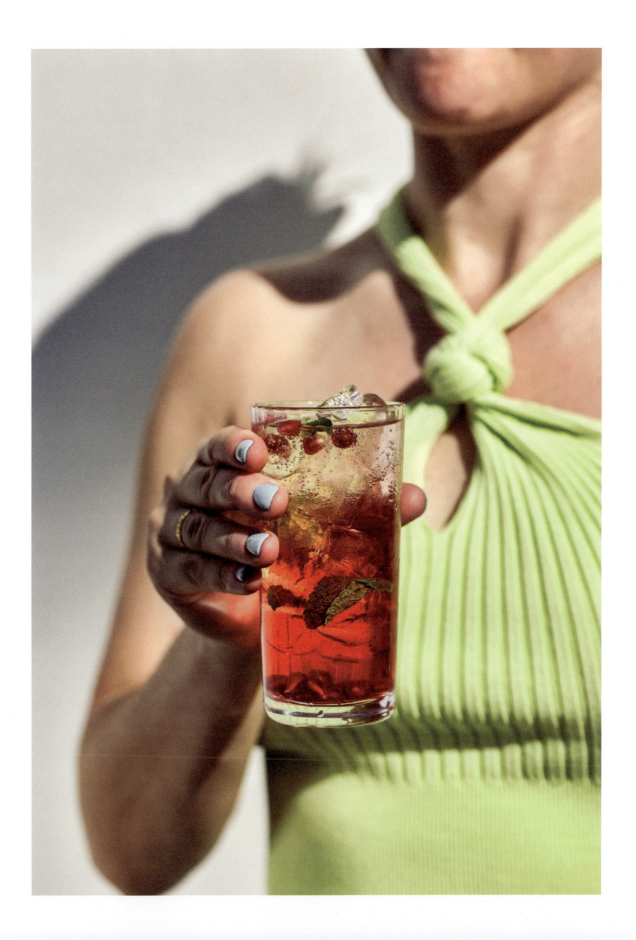

TAVERNA DIARIES

T'APANEMO AMORGOS

AMORGOS

- LOCATION -
Amorgos

- ADDRESS -
Kalofana 840 08, Greece

- PHONE -
+30 2285 072260

- RECIPE -
Psimeni raki

One of the true joys of Greek tavernas is the unexpected connections you make - the people you chat with and the local secrets they generously share. During our time on the island of Tinos, a lively group of locals insisted we visit a small, family run taverna on our upcoming trip to the nearby island of Amorgos. Following their advice, we squeezed a visit to T'APANEMO into our plans, fuelling up for our planned pilgrimage to the awe-inspiring Monastery of Hozoviotissa - and it was an experience we'll never forget.

At T'Apanemo, we were warmly embraced by the Nomikos family, who have run the taverna for just three years, but have poured their hearts into it with dreams of keeping Greece's authentic, time-honoured flavours alive for generations. At the heart of the kitchen, Orania crafts dishes inspired by the seasons, many passed down from her grandmother Kalliopi. Meanwhile, her husband, Kostas, and son, Yiannis, tend the farm that supplies the kitchen with the freshest ingredients, and their three daughters, Paraskevi, Sofia and Kalliopi, welcome guests with a warmth that feels like coming home.

For the family, running a taverna is like welcoming relatives into their home, and the joy of seeing customers leave with satisfied smiles is what makes it all worthwhile. Of course, running a taverna on a remote island like Amorgos - eight hours by ferry from Athens - comes with its challenges. From supply chain hurdles to unpredictable weather (Amorgos is famed for its strong winds) and a limited local workforce, every day brings something new. Yet, for this family, the beauty of their life far outweighs the difficulties. 'Life in the taverna blends tranquillity, vibrancy, companionship and authenticity. It's a daily rhythm focused on simple pleasures - good food, meaningful connections, and a deep bond with nature,' says Orania. Honestly, it sounds like a dream to us.

When it comes to the food, we started with the beef keftedes (meatballs) - perfectly crispy on the outside, yet tender and fluffy on the inside. Orania and Kostas smiled proudly when we asked about them, curious about their secret. 'It's the land it's grown on that makes it so delicious,' they said, referring to their own farm-raised meat. The taverna's specialties include a fragrant lemon-rosemary goat dish, and patatato - a beloved traditional goat and potato stew that's a staple at every wedding and baptism on the island. The menu is a heartfelt tribute to the local and traditional cuisine of Amorgos, crafted around the freshest seasonal ingredients available.

"The menu is a heartfelt tribute to the local and traditional cuisine of Amorgos, crafted around the freshest seasonal ingredients available"

The taverna is also deeply committed to serving as a social hub in the remote southern village of Kolofona, providing a central gathering place for both locals and visitors. The taverna supports local agriculture, livestock farming and other services, while also boosting tourism by offering an authentic and unforgettable dining experience.

For this family, the taverna is more than just a tradition - it's a cherished link to their roots, a way to honour their loved ones, and a means of passing these values and memories to future generations: 'The tradition of tavernas is a significant pillar in preserving our heritage, connected with deep emotional and cultural values from our grandparents. Our taverna is not just a place to eat but a place to share stories, learn about the people who once lived in the village, discover their occupations, and become part of its history.'

Naturally, we couldn't resist asking for a quick recipe, and the family graciously shared their method for psimeni raki - a warm, spiced drink that is a daily staple on Amorgos, and truly captures the essence of the island. We're sure you'll love it during the colder months, too.

Taverna T'Apanemo beautifully embodies the Amorgian tradition of coming together to share stories over a psimeni raki.

PSIMENI RAKI

Serves 6-8

750 ml (3 cups) water
4 cloves
3 cinnamon sticks
2 star anise
1 tablespoon pennyroyal tea leaves
250 g (9 oz) caster (superfine) sugar
375 ml (1½ cups) raki

Pour the water into a large saucepan. Add the spices and tea leaves and bring to the boil over medium heat. Reduce the heat to low and simmer for 30 minutes, until the water is aromatic. Set aside.

Take a large non-stick frying pan and evenly scatter the sugar in the pan. Place over low heat and allow the sugar to melt; this will take 12–15 minutes. Don't touch the pan until the sugar turns golden brown; when it does, use a wooden spoon to carefully give the sugar a mix, to incorporate the remaining sugar.

Remove and discard the spices from the aromatic water and bring back to the boil. Carefully pour the hot water over the sugar, taking care as the sugar will seize up. Using a wooden spoon, gently stir the mixture until the sugar has dissolved.

Add the raki and mix to combine. Cover and allow the mixture to infuse for 24 hours at room temperature.

The following day, serve in small glasses, either cold or warm.

A NOTE ON PREP
You will need to begin this recipe the day before serving, but the best part is, you can make a big batch to have on hand when guests arrive.

If serving the raki cold, transfer to a container and place in the fridge to cool completely. If serving warm, simply reheat the raki in a saucepan over low heat until warm. Make sure not to warm it over high heat or you will cook off the alcohol.

SERVE ME WITH
Good company… or as we say in Greece, parea - close friends who gather together purely to enjoy each other's company and share life experiences.

THANK YOU

This book is dedicated to our beautiful mum, Sophie. Without you we wouldn't be where we are today. Thank you for giving us endless opportunities and forever supporting our next idea or project no matter how big or small it is. We are so lucky to have a mum like you, we love you.

To our beloved Yiayia Koula, we miss you every day. We feel so blessed to have had you in our lives, the knowledge we have today comes from you. You showed us the way in the kitchen from when we were kids to adults. We know how proud you would be of *OPA!*

For those who helped us create *OPA!*: Paul McNally, thank you for giving *Peináo* a sibling. To Lucy and Elena for all your support and wonderful hard work. We appreciate everything you have done for *OPA!* To everyone else at Smith Street Books, thank you for giving us another opportunity to share our love for Greece and its food. Thank you to Gemma Leslie for painting our front cover and chapter openers, you've brought our front cover dreams to life, you're so talented. To George Saad for your delightful book design; and to Sofoklis Nikolis for capturing Greece in such a unique and beautiful way.

To Bonnie, Jess, and Lauren – we are endlessly grateful for the incredible work you put into bringing our vision to life. Your talent and dedication have not only made our recipes shine, but you've also helped us create memories that will stay with us for years to come. We'll always cherish those days spent in our home, arriving in slippers and comfy pants, and gathering around the table to enjoy every dish as it was captured. Thank you, ladies!

To Gina, thank you for sharing your beautiful words and for being such an important part of this journey. Having you in Crete with me (Helena) was so special, thank you for all your support.

To our cousin Alex, thank you for helping translate our taverna stories and for all your love and support.

To all the wonderful taverna owners we had the pleasure of meeting: thank you for welcoming us so warmly and for giving us your time, especially during the busy summer season. We know how crazy things get in hospitality and yet you took moments out of your day to sit with us and share your stories. We'll forever cherish these conversations and the kindness you showed us.

Niko, thank you for allowing us to shoot at your papou's house (let's hope he doesn't read this) and for delivering us coffee and hot cheesy pita every morning. Your hard work and support means the world to us, and we can't thank you enough for everything you've done.

To our friends Angela, Emma, Chloe, Sophia, Rachael, Nicole, Anastasia and Ryan thank you for always supporting us. We are so lucky to have such incredible friends like you.

THANK YOU

VIKKI WOULD LIKE TO THANK …

To my Billie, everything mummy does is for you. I count my blessings every day, I love you so much Billie mou. To my wonderful husband, Luke, thank you for allowing me to chase every opportunity and dream that comes my way. You really are the best dad and husband! To Helena, thank you for all your hard work travelling to Greece to bring the tavernas to life, all the stories and photos are so beautiful to read and without you we wouldn't have got it done.

HELENA WOULD LIKE TO THANK …

Mum, thank you for being my assistant and translator throughout our Greece trip. I couldn't have managed everything without you there to help make it all possible. From work to exploring, you made it all easier and so much more enjoyable. I know you loved this trip just as much as I did.

To Niko, thank you for your endless love and support throughout the process of writing *OPA!* Thank you for having my back, running to the shops when I needed to find a specific ingredient, and for tasting my recipes a thousand times until I was happy. You helped me in ways that I am forever grateful for. I love you x

AND SPECIAL THANKS TO …

The Harris Farm team for keeping the fridge and pantry well stocked – thank you!

Lamia Super Deli in Marrickville, Sydney, thank you for letting us shoot in your beautiful store.

Peter from Northside Seafood for providing the freshest seafood and delivering it to our doorstep.

Krystal from the Greek Providore for sharing all your beautiful hand-picked Greek products with us.

Georgie Dolling for her beautiful props and plates.

George from Melvourni Coffee.

Michael from Sam's MFC Supermarket in Rosebery, Sydney, where we got a lot of our Greek ingredients.

Vicky from Hellenic Wines and Spirits for supplying us with Skinos Mastiha.

INDEX

A

almonds
    Dark chocolate-coated almond clusters 212
    Spiced almond & pistachio kataifi 211
artichokes, Eggs with artichoke & tomato 56
aubergines *see* eggplants
Avgolemono 75, 190

B

Baked chickpeas 140
Baked feta with tomato & peppers 48
Bamies 184
Barbounia tiganita 76
basil, The Med 235
Bechamel 149
beef
    Beef pastitsio with graviera bechamel 145
    Beef stifado with baby whole onions 156
    Biftekia 114
    Bolognese sauce 145
    Cabbage rolls with avgolemono 190
    Pork & beef meatballs in tomato sauce 155
    Soutzoukakia on the grill 126
Beetroot with mizithra cheese 177
Biftekia with tzatziki 114
biscuits
    Greek chocolate slice 202
    Olive oil & orange biscuits 206
Black-eyed bean salad 172
black olives
    Black olive village bread 59
    Dakos salad 178

Blood orange & shallot vinaigrette 28
Bolognese sauce 145
Bouyiourdi 48
bread
    Black olive village bread 59
    Dakos salad 178
    Grilled sardines & tomato on charred bread 84
    Rye confit garlic taramosalata 22
    see also pita bread
bucatini, Beef pastitsio with graviera bechamel 145
butters
    Fennel & caper butter 72
    Roasted pepper butter 108

C

Cabbage rolls with avgolemono 190
cakes
    Lemon yoghurt cake 205
    Walnut syrup cake 208
calamari, Grilled calamari with fava & pickled onion 78
caperberries
    Grilled calamari with fava & pickled onions 78
    Octopus with caperberries & lemon 68
capsicums *see* peppers
carrots, Fisherman's soup 88
celery, Black-eyed bean salad 172
cheeses 15
    see also feta, galotyri, graviera, haloumi, kasseri, kefalotyri, manouri, mizithra
chervil, Lettuce salad 171

chicken
    Chicken souvlaki with Greek fries 106
    Hilopites with chicken 152
    Honey chicken wings with galotyri & green pepper herby oil 118
    Preserved lemon roasted chicken with jammy leeks 146
chickpeas
    Baked chickpeas 140
    Chickpea fritters with minty yoghurt 42
chocolate
    Dark chocolate-coated almond clusters 212
    Greek chocolate slice 202
Clams with lemon rice 99
cocktails
    Ouzo & olive oil sour 236
    Pomegranate & mint spritz 238
    The Med 235
coffee
    Frappe 232
    The perfect Greek coffee 230
Confit garlic oil 26
courgettes *see* zucchini
cucumbers
    Loukaniko with white onion & cucumbers 111
    Tzatziki 114

D

Dakos salad 178
Dark chocolate-coated almond clusters 212
dill
    Black-eyed bean salad 172
    Greens pie 183
    Herby potato salad 174
    Lettuce salad 171

INDEX

dips
  Rye confit garlic taramosalata 22
  Spicy cheese dip 20
  Tzatziki 114
Dolmades 31
dressings
  Blood orange & shallot vinaigrette 28
  Lemon dressing 168

E

eggplants
  Eggplant & roasted red peppers 25
  Eggplant topped with lamb mince & bechamel 149
  Fennel-seed fried zucchini & eggplant 60
eggs
  Eggs with artichoke & tomato 56
  Potato & eggs with graviera 40

F

Fava 78
fennel
  Fennel & caper butter 72
  Fennel-seed fried zucchini & eggplant 60
  Fisherman's soup 88
  Prawn stock 96
feta
  Baked feta with tomato & peppers 48
  Dakos salad 178
  Filo-fried feta with honey & nuts 46
  Greek fries with goat's feta & oregano 34
  Greens pie 183
  Mussel saganaki with red peppers 94
  Okra with tomatoes 184
  Peppers stuffed with Greek cheeses & sun-dried tomato 142
  Spicy cheese dip 20
  Village salad 168
figs
  Jammy figs with honey & yoghurt 196
  Sticky fig & honey semifreddo 219
filo pastry
  Filo-fried feta with honey & nuts 46
  Milk custard pie 200
fish
  Fisherman's soup 88
  Fried red mullet 76
  Fried whitebait with ouzo mayonnaise 66
  Grilled sardines & tomato on charred bread 84
  Sardines with tomato & marjoram 71
  Snapper with avgolemono & charred horta 75
  Swordfish with roasted grapes & green olive salsa 87
  Tuna with blood orange & shallot vinaigrette 28
  see also seafood
Fisherman's soup 88
Frappe 232
Fried red mullet 76
Fried whitebait with ouzo mayonnaise 66
fritters, Chickpea fritters with minty yoghurt 42

G

Galaktoboureko with walnuts 200
galotyri 15
  Honey chicken wings with galotyri & green pepper herby oil 118
garlic
  Confit garlic oil 26
  Rye confit garlic taramosalata 22
Gigantes plaki 134
gin, Pomegranate & mint spritz 238
Glyko tou koutaliou 220
Goat in olive oil 162
goat's cheese, Peppers stuffed with Greek cheeses & sun-dried tomato 142
granita, Sour cherry & vermouth granita 215
grapes
  Grape spoon sweet 220
  Swordfish with roasted grapes & green olive salsa 87
graviera 15
  Graviera bechamel 145
  Potato & eggs with graviera 40
Greek chocolate slice 202
Greek coffee, The perfect Greek coffee 230
Greek fries with goat's feta & oregano 34
Greek giant baked beans 134
Greek pantry 12–15
green olives
  Green olive salsa 87
  Stuffed fried olives 45
Green pepper herby oil 118
Greens pie 183
Grilled calamari with fava & pickled onion 78
Grilled lamb's liver with onions 120
Grilled sardines & tomato on charred bread 84

H

haloumi 15
Herb marinade 117
herbs 14
Herby potato salad 174
Hilopites with chicken 152
honey
  Filo-fried feta with honey & nuts 46
  Honey & orange syrup 208
  Honey chicken wings with galotyri & green pepper herby oil 118
  Honey puffs with pistachio 199
  Jammy figs with honey & yoghurt 196
  Sticky fig & honey semifreddo 219
Horiatiki salata 168
Horiatiko psomi 59
horta (wild greens), Snapper with avgolemono & charred horta 75
Hortopita 183
Htapodi me makaronaki kofto 90

J

Jammy figs with honey & yoghurt 196
Jazzmin (taverna), Amorgos 226–9

K

Kagianas 56
Kakavia 88
Karidopita 208
kasseri 15
  Stuffed fried olives 45
kataifi pastry, Spiced almond & pistachio kataifi 211
Katsikaki tsigariasto 162

kefalotyri 15
    Baked feta with tomato & peppers 48
    Bechamel 149
    Beef pastitsio with graviera bechamel 145
    Eggplant topped with lamb mince & bechamel 149
King prawns with fennel & caper butter 72
Kolokithakia kai melitzanes tiganites 60

L

Ladokouloura 206
Lahabodolmades 190
lamb
    Eggplant topped with lamb mince & bechamel 149
    Lamb chops with pickled pepper & shallot 117
    Lamb kleftiko with roasted tomatoes & potatoes 150
    Lamb-stuffed vine leaves 31
lamb's liver, Grilled lamb's liver with onions 120
leeks, Preserved lemon roasted chicken with jammy leeks 146
legumes 14
lemons 14
    Avgolemono 75
    Grape spoon sweet 220
    Lemon & oregano marinade 150
    Lemon & oregano oil 112
    Lemon dressing 168
    Lemon potatoes 180
    Lemon syrup 200, 205
    Lemon yoghurt cake 205
    Octopus with caperberries & lemon 68
    Ouzo & olive oil sour 236
    see also preserved lemon
lima beans, Greek giant baked beans 134
Loukaniko with white onion & cucumbers 111
Loukoumades 199

M

mandarins, Ouzo & citrus sorbet 216
manouri 15
marinades
    Herb marinade 117
    Lemon & oregano marinade 150
marjoram, Sardines with tomato & marjoram 71
Maroulosalata 171
mayonnaise, Ouzo mayonnaise 66
meatballs
    Pork & beef meatballs in tomato sauce 155
    Soutzoukakia on the grill 126
Melitzanosalata 25
Milk custard pie 200
mint
    Greens pie 183
    Minty yoghurt 42
    Pomegranate & mint spritz 238
mizithra 15
    Beetroot with mizithra cheese 177
Mosaiko 202
mussels
    Fisherman's soup 88
    Mussel saganaki with red peppers 94

N

Ntounias (taverna), Crete 158–61
nuts, Filo-fried feta with honey & nuts 46

O

octopus
    Octopus with caperberries & lemon 68
    Red wine octopus with small pasta 90
oils
    Confit garlic oil 26
    Green pepper herby oil 118
    Lemon & oregano oil 112
    see also dressings; mayonnaise; vinaigrette
Okra with tomatoes 184
olive oil 12
    Goat in olive oil 162
    Olive oil & orange biscuits 206
    Ouzo & olive oil sour 236

olives 13
    Village salad 168
    see also black olives; green olives
onions
    Beef stifado with baby whole onions 156
    Grilled calamari with fava & pickled onion 78
    Grilled lamb's liver with onions 120
    Loukaniko with white onion & cucumbers 111
oranges
    Honey & orange syrup 208
    Olive oil & orange biscuits 206
    Ouzo & citrus sorbet 216
    The Med 235
oregano 14
    Dakos salad 178
    Greek fries with goat's feta & oregano 34
    Lemon & oregano marinade 150
    Lemon & oregano oil 112
    Pork spare ribs with lemon & oregano 112
    Prawn youvetsi 96
    Snapper with avgolemono & charred horta 75
ouzo
    Ouzo & citrus sorbet 216
    Ouzo & olive oil sour 236
    Ouzo mayonnaise 66

P

Papoutsakia 149
parsley
    Beetroot with mizithra cheese 177
    Black-eyed bean salad 172
    Cabbage rolls with avgolemono 190
pasta
    Beef pastitsio with graviera bechamel 145
    Hilopites with chicken 152
    Prawn youvetsi 96
    Red wine octopus with small pasta 90
    Scampi spaghetti with confit tomato 93
pastry
    Greens pie 183
    see also filo pastry; kataifi pastry
Patates lemonates 180
Patates me avga 40
Patates tiganites 34
Patatosalata 174

INDEX

pepperoncini
  Green pepper herby oil 118
  Pickled pepper & shallot 117
  Village salad 168
peppers
  Baked feta with tomato & peppers 48
  Eggplant & roasted red peppers 25
  Greek giant baked beans 134
  Mussel saganaki with red peppers 94
  Peppers stuffed with Greek cheeses & sun-dried tomato 142
  Roasted pepper butter 108
The perfect Greek coffee 230
Pickled pepper & shallot 117
pies
  Greens pie 183
  Milk custard pie 200
pistachios
  Honey puffs with pistachio 199
  Spiced almond & pistachio kataifi 211
pita bread 12
  Eggplant & roasted red peppers 25
  Pita breads with confit garlic oil 26
Pomegranate & mint spritz 238
pork
  Biftekia 114
  Pork & beef meatballs in tomato sauce 155
  Pork chops with roasted pepper butter 108
  Pork spare ribs with lemon & oregano 112
  Soutzoukakia on the grill 126
potatoes
  Chicken souvlaki with Greek fries 106
  Fisherman's soup 88
  Greek fries with goat's feta & oregano 34
  Herby potato salad 174
  Lamb kleftiko with roasted tomatoes & potatoes 150
  Lemon potatoes 180
  Potato & eggs with graviera 40
prawns
  King prawns with fennel & caper butter 72
  Prawn stock 96
  Prawn youvetsi 96
Preserved lemon roasted chicken with jammy leeks 146
Psimeni raki 244

R

raki, Psimeni raki 244
red wine
  Beef stifado with baby whole onions 156
  Bolognese sauce 145
  Red wine octopus with small pasta 90
red wine vinegar 12
  Octopus with caperberries & lemon 68
Revithada 140
Revithokeftedes 42
rice
  Cabbage rolls with avgolemono 190
  Clams with lemon rice 99
  Lamb-stuffed vine leaves 31
  Rice-stuffed zucchini flowers 133
risoni, Prawn youvetsi 96
Roasted pepper butter 108
Rye confit garlic taramosalata 22

S

salads
  Beetroot with mizithra cheese 177
  Black-eyed bean salad 172
  Dakos salad 178
  Herby potato salad 174
  Lettuce salad 171
  Village salad 168
salsas, Green olive salsa 87
salt 12
sardines
  Grilled sardines & tomato on charred bread 84
  Sardines with tomato & marjoram 71
sauces
  Avgolemono 75, 190
  Bechamel 149
  Bolognese sauce 145
  Graviera bechamel 145
  Tomato sauce 155
Scampi spaghetti with confit tomato 93
seafood
  Clams with lemon rice 99
  Fisherman's soup 88
  Grilled calamari with fava & pickled onion 78
  King prawns with fennel & caper butter 72
  Mussel saganaki with red peppers 94
  Octopus with caperberries & lemon 68
  Prawn youvetsi 96

Red wine octopus with small pasta 90
  Scampi spaghetti with confit tomato 93
semifreddo, Sticky fig & honey semifreddo 219
shallots
  Blood orange & shallot vinaigrette 28
  Pickled pepper & shallot 117
silverbeet, Greek giant baked beans 134
Skinos Mastiha Spirit, The Med 235
Snapper with avgolemono & charred horta 75
sorbets, Ouzo & citrus sorbet 216
soup, Fisherman's soup 88
Sour cherry & vermouth granita 215
Soutzoukakia 155
Soutzoukakia on the grill 126
souvlaki, Chicken souvlaki with Greek fries 106
spaghetti, Scampi spaghetti with confit tomato 93
Spiced almond & pistachio kataifi 211
Spicy cheese dip 20
spinach, Greens pie 183
split peas, Fava 78
spring onions
  Beetroot with mizithra cheese 177
  Black-eyed bean salad 172
  Herby potato salad 174
  Lettuce salad 171
Sta Fys' Aera (taverna), Tinos 52-5
Sticky fig & honey semifreddo 219
Stuffed fried olives 45
sun-dried tomatoes, Peppers stuffed with Greek cheeses & sun-dried tomato 142
Swordfish with roasted grapes & green olive salsa 87
syrups 211
  Honey & orange syrup 208
  Lemon syrup 200, 205

T

T'Apenemo Amorgos (taverna), Amorgos 240-3
tarama caviar, Rye confit garlic taramosalata 22
Taverna Kronos, Thsessaloniki 122-5
Taverna Oikonomou (taverna), Athens 186-9
Taverna Tou Charis, Naxos 36-9
The Med 235
Tirokafteri 20
To Steki Tou Machera (taverna), Amorgos 136-9

tomatoes
 Baked chickpeas 140
 Baked feta with tomato & peppers 48
 Beef stifado with baby whole onions 156
 Dakos salad 178
 Eggplant topped with lamb mince & bechamel 149
 Eggs with artichoke & tomato 56
 Fisherman's soup 88
 Greek giant baked beans 134
 Grilled sardines & tomato on charred bread 84
 Lamb kleftiko with roasted tomatoes & potatoes 150
 Lamb-stuffed vine leaves 31
 Mussel saganaki with red peppers 94
 Okra with tomatoes 184
 Red wine octopus with small pasta 90
 Rice-stuffed zucchini flowers 133
 Sardines with tomato & marjoram 71
 Scampi spaghetti with confit tomato 93
 Tomato sauce 155
 Village salad 168
 see also sun-dried tomatoes
Tuna with blood orange & shallot vinaigrette 28
Tzatziki 114

V

vermouth, Sour cherry & vermouth granita 215
Village salad 168
vinaigrette, Blood orange & shallot vinaigrette 28
vine leaves, Lamb-stuffed vine leaves 31
vinegar 12

W

walnuts
 Milk custard pie 200
 Walnut syrup cake 208
white wine
 Clams with lemon rice 99
 Goat in olive oil 162
 Mussel saganaki with red peppers 94
whitebait, Fried whitebait with ouzo mayonnaise 66

Y

Yiaourtopita 205
yoghurt
 Greens pie 183
 Jammy figs with honey & yoghurt 196
 Lemon yoghurt cake 205
 Minty yoghurt 42
 Spicy cheese dip 20
 Tzatziki 114
Yperokeanio (taverna), Athens 80–3

Z

zucchini, Fennel-seed fried zucchini & eggplant 60
zucchini flowers, Rice-stuffed zucchini flowers 133

Published in 2025 by Smith Street Books
Naarm (Melbourne) | Australia
smithstreetbooks.com

Distributed outside of ANZ, North & Latin America by
Thames & Hudson Ltd., 6–24 Britannia Street, London, WC1X 9JD
thamesandhudson.com

EU Authorised Representative: Interart S.A.R.L.
19 rue Charles Auray, 93500 Pantin, Paris, France
productsafety@thameshudson.co.uk; www.interart.fr

ISBN: 978-1-9232-3918-0

All rights reserved. No part of this book may be reproduced or transmitted by any person or entity, in any form or by any means, electronic or mechanical, including photocopying, recording, scanning or by any storage and retrieval system, without the prior written permission of the publishers and copyright holders.

Smith Street Books respectfully acknowledges the Wurundjeri People of the Kulin Nation, who are the Traditional Owners of the land on which we work, and we pay our respects to their Elders past and present.

Copyright text © Helena and Vikki Moursellas
Copyright design © Smith Street Books
Copyright photography © Bonnie Coumbe, excluding
p. 4, 7 (top), 8, (bottom row), 11 (top row), 19 (left), 50, 54, 55, 57, 65 (left), 100, 101, 105 (right), 124, 125, 127, 131, 138, 139, 141, 167, 188, 189, 191, 194 (left), 195, 224, 228, 229, 231, 242, 243, 245, 247 (right), 255 (top) © Sofoklis Nikolis, and
p. 7 (bottom), 8 (top), 11 (bottom), 38, 39, 41, 51, 64, 65 (right), 82, 83, 85, 105 (left), 130, 160, 161, 163, 166, 194 (right), 197, 246, 247 (left) © Helena Moursellas
Copyright cover and chapter opener paintings © Gemma Leslie

The moral rights of the authors have been asserted.

Publisher: Paul McNally
Managing editor: Lucy Heaver
Project editor: Elena Callcott
Editor: Katri Hilden
Design: George Saad
Cover and chapter opener paintings: Gemma Leslie
Food photographer: Bonnie Coumbe
Food stylist: Jess Johnson
Prop stylist: Lauren Miller
Photo chefs: Helena and Vikki Moursellas
Taverna and location photographers: Sofoklis Nikolis and Helena Moursellas
Travel and culture writer: Gina Lionatos
Proofreader: Pamela Dunne
Indexer: Max McMaster
Layout and pre-press: Megan Ellis
Production manager: Aisling Coughlan

Printed & bound in China by C&C Offset Printing Co., Ltd.

Book 401
10 9 8 7 6 5 4 3 2 1